QUIC:
Revolutionizing Internet Transport

James Relington

DEDICATION

To those who seek knowledge, inspiration, and new perspectives—
may this book be a companion on your journey, a spark for curiosity,
and a reminder that every page turned is a step toward discovery.

AKNOWLEDGEMENTS

I would like to express my deepest gratitude to everyone who contributed to the creation of this book. To my colleagues and mentors, your insights and expertise have been invaluable. A special thank you to my family and friends for their unwavering support and encouragement throughout this journey.

The Dawn of Internet Transport Protocols

The story of internet transport protocols begins in the late 1960s and early 1970s, an era when computer networks were experimental and fragmented. Researchers and engineers were working tirelessly to connect disparate systems across large distances, leading to the creation of the ARPANET, one of the world's first packet-switched networks. The need for a standard way to move data reliably between computers became evident as these networks grew in size and complexity. In response to this challenge, the foundational layers of what would become the modern internet began to take shape, with a focus on creating robust transport protocols that could operate in a variety of environments and across diverse hardware.

The initial efforts were guided by the principle of reliability. Computers and networks at the time were inherently unreliable, and the risk of data loss due to congestion, hardware failure, or line noise was high. The first major step toward solving this problem came in the form of the Network Control Protocol (NCP), used on the ARPANET. NCP introduced rudimentary mechanisms for flow control and multiplexing, but it lacked key features needed to ensure end-to-end reliability across a growing and evolving network. As demands increased and more diverse use cases emerged, it became clear that a more sophisticated approach was necessary.

By the mid-1970s, the need for a more universal and scalable transport layer protocol was driving the work of researchers like Vint Cerf and Bob Kahn. Their collaboration led to the invention of the Transmission Control Protocol (TCP), a revolutionary concept that introduced core mechanisms such as reliable byte streams, retransmission of lost packets, congestion control, and flow control. TCP was designed to create a virtual circuit between endpoints, providing an abstraction where applications could communicate as if they were using a direct, reliable channel, even when the underlying network was chaotic or unreliable.

TCP's success lay in its ability to adapt to network conditions dynamically. By adjusting the rate at which data was sent based on congestion signals, TCP could operate across a wide variety of network topologies, from slow dial-up lines to emerging broadband connections. It quickly became the backbone of early internet communications, underpinning the World Wide Web, email systems, file transfers, and countless other services that defined the digital revolution of the 1990s and 2000s.

However, TCP did not emerge in isolation. Alongside it, another protocol was developed to address a different set of needs. The User Datagram Protocol (UDP) was introduced as a simpler, connectionless counterpart to TCP. Unlike TCP, UDP provided a best-effort delivery model with no guarantees of packet delivery, ordering, or error correction. This simplicity made UDP ideal for applications where speed and low latency were more important than reliability, such as Domain Name System (DNS) queries, streaming media, and real-time gaming.

The coexistence of TCP and UDP formed the transport layer foundation for most internet applications. Together, they offered a spectrum of options: TCP for reliability and ordered delivery, UDP for speed and flexibility. Both protocols relied on the Internet Protocol (IP) to move packets across networks, establishing the fundamental model of internet transport that persists to this day. Yet, as the internet continued to grow and evolve, cracks in this foundation began to show.

TCP, while reliable, was often criticized for its inefficiencies, particularly in environments where latency and packet loss were prevalent, such as mobile networks or satellite links. Its head-of-line blocking behavior, where a single lost packet could delay all subsequent packets in a stream, became a significant bottleneck for web performance. UDP, while faster, left the burden of reliability and congestion control entirely on the application layer, resulting in fragmented and inconsistent implementations across different systems.

Despite these challenges, TCP and UDP remained largely unchallenged for decades. They became deeply embedded in network stacks, middleboxes, firewalls, and routers, shaping the internet's infrastructure. Efforts to evolve transport protocols were hampered by the ossification of the internet, a phenomenon where widely deployed systems and intermediary devices restricted the deployment of new protocols or significant changes to existing ones.

Even so, the growing demands of modern web applications, streaming services, and mobile usage pushed researchers and engineers to question whether the status quo was sufficient. The explosion of video conferencing, online gaming, and cloud computing highlighted the limitations of traditional transport protocols, particularly in an era where user expectations for speed, reliability, and security were higher than ever before.

The groundwork laid by TCP and UDP was critical. These protocols proved that scalable, global communication was possible, and they enabled the rise of the internet as a transformative force in society. However, they were products of a different time, designed under constraints that no longer aligned with the needs of the modern internet. As such, the stage was set for a new generation of transport protocols to emerge, one that could build on the lessons of the past while addressing the evolving realities of today's interconnected world.

The dawn of internet transport protocols was more than just the creation of technical standards; it was the birth of a philosophy centered on open, interoperable, and resilient communication. TCP and UDP not only enabled communication across continents but also democratized access to information and services. Their legacy persists, even as the world moves toward newer technologies designed to meet the demands of a fast-paced, mobile-first, and security-conscious digital landscape. The revolution that began with NCP, TCP, and UDP has paved the way for innovations like QUIC, which promises to redefine what transport protocols can achieve.

The Limitations of TCP and UDP

As the internet matured and diversified, the foundational transport protocols TCP and UDP began to show their age. Though they played a pivotal role in the success and scalability of the early internet, both protocols were designed under assumptions and conditions very different from those faced by modern applications and networks. The global internet had transformed into a dynamic and highly varied environment, connecting billions of devices across wired and wireless networks, traversing middleboxes, firewalls, and an increasingly complex web of routing infrastructures. Under such circumstances, the shortcomings of TCP and UDP became more apparent, and their limitations posed significant obstacles to further innovation and performance optimization.

TCP, the more feature-rich of the two, was lauded for its reliability and ordered delivery. It provided a stream abstraction that ensured data arrived intact and in sequence, making it ideal for applications like file transfers, email, and early web browsing. However, this reliability came at a cost. TCP's most notorious limitation is its head-of-line blocking problem. Because TCP delivers data as an ordered byte stream, the loss of a single packet forces the receiver to halt the processing of subsequent packets until the missing data is retransmitted and received. In high-latency or lossy networks, such as mobile connections or satellite links, this behavior can introduce significant delays, degrading user experience. In modern web applications where numerous resources are loaded concurrently, head-of-line blocking at the transport layer can severely impact page load times and responsiveness.

Another major issue with TCP is its connection establishment process. The standard TCP handshake requires three round-trip messages to fully establish a connection before data transfer can begin. In latency-sensitive environments, such as mobile networks where signal quality fluctuates, these extra round trips can noticeably delay communications. Efforts to address this, such as TCP Fast Open, have provided some relief, but deployment and adoption have been inconsistent due to concerns about middlebox compatibility and security.

TCP's built-in congestion control mechanisms, while effective in many scenarios, were not originally designed with today's network diversity in mind. The classic algorithms, such as TCP Reno and TCP Cubic, often struggle to fully utilize available bandwidth on high-speed, high-latency networks while avoiding congestion in low-capacity environments. This one-size-fits-all approach leads to underutilization or, conversely, network congestion and packet loss, neither of which aligns well with the demands of modern applications like video conferencing, cloud gaming, or large-scale data transfers.

On the other hand, UDP's design sacrifices reliability for speed. By providing a minimal, connectionless transport mechanism, UDP allows applications to send datagrams without waiting for handshakes or acknowledgments. This model enables lower latency communications, making UDP an attractive choice for real-time applications such as VoIP, live video streaming, and online multiplayer games. However, the lack of built-in mechanisms for packet loss recovery, flow control, or congestion avoidance places the burden of these responsibilities on the application layer. Developers must implement custom solutions to handle issues like packet reordering, retransmission, and network congestion, resulting in significant engineering complexity and the potential for fragmented, inconsistent implementations.

UDP's simplicity also leads to problems when interacting with the modern internet's ecosystem of middleboxes, firewalls, and network address translators (NATs). Many network devices are optimized for TCP traffic and may restrict, throttle, or block UDP packets entirely. This behavior introduces unpredictability and restricts UDP's effectiveness in certain environments, especially corporate or highly regulated networks where security policies favor TCP traffic. Even when UDP traffic is permitted, NAT traversal techniques like STUN and TURN must often be employed to establish reliable peer-to-peer connections, adding further latency and complexity to real-time applications.

Security is another area where TCP and UDP show their age. Both protocols were designed at a time when the internet was a more trusted and academic environment. As a result, they lack native encryption and depend on external protocols like TLS or DTLS to provide confidentiality and integrity. While these protocols are widely used and trusted, they add additional handshake steps, overhead, and deployment challenges. Moreover, combining these security layers with TCP or UDP is not always seamless. For example, TLS over TCP suffers from compounded latency due to the dual handshakes required by both protocols, a noticeable drawback for modern applications prioritizing speed and user experience.

Both TCP and UDP also suffer from limited extensibility. Over the years, attempts to enhance TCP with new features or performance improvements have been consistently hampered by ossification. The internet's infrastructure, filled with legacy equipment and conservative middleboxes, tends to block or interfere with non-standard TCP options or unfamiliar protocol behaviors. As a result, innovative enhancements to TCP's capabilities, such as Multipath TCP or advanced congestion control algorithms, face deployment hurdles, leading to slow adoption and uneven support across networks.

The reality is that both TCP and UDP were designed for a different era, one where wired connections dominated, and networks were relatively stable and homogenous. Today's internet is mobile-centric, distributed, and security-conscious, demanding transport protocols that can seamlessly adapt to changing network conditions, minimize latency, and integrate security by design. Modern applications require high-performance transport mechanisms that can support multiplexed streams, tolerate packet loss gracefully, and reduce connection establishment times without sacrificing security or compatibility.

Despite these limitations, TCP and UDP remain the workhorses of the internet, deeply ingrained in operating systems, network devices, and application architectures. Their longevity is a testament to their simplicity and effectiveness in many use cases, but the growing demands of today's digital ecosystem have exposed their constraints. These limitations have spurred the development of new transport protocols that seek to blend the reliability of TCP with the speed and flexibility of UDP, while also incorporating modern security features and performance optimizations.

The shortcomings of TCP and UDP have served as a catalyst for innovation, motivating engineers and researchers to reimagine what a modern transport protocol should look like. It is against this backdrop that new protocols like QUIC have emerged, aiming to overcome the historical challenges of traditional transport layers and deliver faster, more reliable, and secure communications for the next generation of internet applications.

The Need for Speed: Why QUIC Emerged

The internet's exponential growth and the changing expectations of its users created the perfect storm for a new transport protocol to emerge. The modern web is no longer the static collection of text-based pages it once was. Today, it is a vibrant ecosystem of dynamic content, rich multimedia, real-time communications, and interactive applications, all demanding speed, responsiveness, and seamless user experience. As web applications grew more sophisticated, so did the frustration with the underlying transport protocols that had powered the internet for decades. TCP and UDP, despite their foundational roles, could no longer keep up with the relentless pursuit of faster, more secure, and more reliable data transfer. The limitations were not merely technical inconveniences; they translated into slower websites, buffering videos, laggy video calls, and ultimately dissatisfied users. It was within this context that QUIC emerged—not just as an incremental improvement but as a rethinking of how transport should work in the internet's new era.

The early 2010s were a pivotal period when mobile internet usage began to overtake desktop, and applications like video streaming, online gaming, and real-time collaboration tools became the norm. These services required low-latency connections and the ability to recover gracefully from network disruptions. Mobile networks introduced further complexity with their higher latency, frequent packet loss, and constant IP address changes due to cellular handoffs. TCP's inherent limitations, like head-of-line blocking and its multi-round-trip handshake, were increasingly viewed as bottlenecks in this landscape. Each additional millisecond spent establishing a connection or recovering from a lost packet could spell the difference between a smooth experience and user abandonment.

Meanwhile, web companies like Google were keenly aware of the direct link between latency and user engagement. Even minor delays in page load times could result in measurable drops in user retention and conversion rates. Speed was not merely a technical goal; it was a business imperative. Google, in particular, had already been experimenting with techniques to optimize web performance, including efforts to reduce TCP connection setup times and streamline TLS handshakes. Yet, each optimization bumped into the same hard ceiling: the legacy constraints of TCP and its entanglement with the ossified internet infrastructure.

The ossification of the internet posed a unique challenge. Over the years, the wide deployment of middleboxes—firewalls, NATs, and deep packet inspection systems—had made it increasingly difficult to introduce changes to TCP or to deploy entirely new transport protocols. These intermediary devices were programmed to recognize and manage familiar traffic patterns, blocking or modifying anything that deviated from standard behaviors. As a result, attempts to roll out improved transport mechanisms frequently met resistance from the very fabric of the internet itself.

It was against this backdrop that QUIC, originally conceived by Google engineers, took shape. The insight was to leverage UDP, which remained relatively unencumbered by middlebox interference due to its simplicity and lack of built-in congestion control or flow management. By building QUIC on top of UDP, developers could effectively bypass many of the legacy obstacles that plagued TCP innovation. This approach allowed QUIC to be deployed incrementally at the application level, rather than requiring kernel-level changes or modifications to network infrastructure, accelerating its adoption in production environments.

But speed was not just about reducing round trips. QUIC was designed to address multiple pain points simultaneously. One of its hallmark innovations was the integration of cryptographic handshakes into the transport layer itself. Unlike the traditional model where TLS sat atop TCP, QUIC merged transport and security, enabling encrypted connections to be established with fewer round trips. In many cases, QUIC could achieve zero-round-trip time (0-RTT) for resumed connections, allowing data to flow almost immediately after initiating a session. This tight coupling of transport and encryption significantly reduced connection establishment latency while enhancing security, making encryption the default rather than an optional layer.

Beyond connection setup speed, QUIC's multiplexing capabilities solved another critical problem: the head-of-line blocking inherent in

TCP. By allowing multiple independent streams to coexist within a single QUIC connection, packet loss on one stream no longer blocked the delivery of data on others. This was particularly impactful for HTTP/2 workloads, where browsers often needed to download dozens or hundreds of resources in parallel. With QUIC, individual streams could fail or recover without holding up unrelated streams, smoothing out the performance of complex web applications and improving the perceived responsiveness for end users.

Another key driver behind QUIC's emergence was the need for transport protocols to be more agile and adaptable to modern network conditions. Unlike TCP, whose congestion control algorithms were constrained by ossified implementations and middlebox expectations, QUIC was designed to be extensible and to evolve rapidly. Because it operates in user space rather than the kernel, QUIC implementations could experiment with and deploy new congestion control strategies without requiring system-wide updates or reconfiguration of network devices. This flexibility enabled faster iteration cycles and the ability to tailor congestion control behaviors to the specific needs of different applications and environments.

QUIC also introduced native support for connection migration, allowing active sessions to survive changes in network conditions, such as a mobile device switching from Wi-Fi to cellular data. This feature significantly reduced the disruptions that users experienced when transitioning between networks, especially on mobile devices where network switching is commonplace.

Ultimately, QUIC emerged out of necessity. The internet had evolved dramatically, but the protocols that powered it had not kept pace. The hunger for speed, security, and resilience drove engineers to rethink old assumptions and develop a transport protocol suited for the modern web. QUIC was not just a technical solution to TCP's shortcomings; it was a response to the growing demands of users who expect instant access, real-time interaction, and flawless performance in an increasingly mobile and bandwidth-hungry world.

In this sense, QUIC represents a turning point. It reflects a broader shift towards protocols that are agile, secure by default, and capable of delivering the responsiveness and reliability demanded by the applications and services of today and tomorrow. Its emergence signaled that the internet community was ready to challenge decades-old conventions in favor of innovation and adaptability.

Google's Experimental Beginnings

The origins of QUIC can be traced back to the early 2010s inside the engineering corridors of Google, where the relentless pursuit of performance optimization was already embedded in the company's culture. At this time, Google was a dominant force on the web, serving billions of users daily through its search engine, YouTube, Gmail, and an ever-growing ecosystem of applications and services. With such scale came a unique vantage point. Google was acutely aware of how even small improvements in speed and efficiency could yield massive benefits in user engagement and resource utilization. The company had long been focused on web performance, contributing to standards like SPDY, an experimental protocol designed to optimize HTTP. Yet even with such efforts, it became increasingly clear to Google's engineers that the root of many performance bottlenecks lay deeper in the stack—within the transport layer itself.

The engineers at Google were constantly monitoring and analyzing real-world user data. This telemetry provided evidence that the limitations of TCP, particularly in mobile and congested networks, were materially affecting user experience. For years, Google had implemented workarounds at the application layer, attempting to hide latency through aggressive caching, connection pooling, and speculative connections. While these techniques offered some relief, they were patchwork solutions to a much deeper problem. TCP's aging design and the latency introduced by traditional TLS handshakes were limiting factors that no amount of client-side optimization could fully overcome.

This led to a critical realization inside Google: a fundamental rethinking of the transport layer was needed to achieve the next leap in web performance. Around 2012, a small group of engineers began exploring what would eventually become QUIC. Initially, the project was shrouded in internal experimentation, an ambitious attempt to design a transport protocol that would provide the speed and reliability the modern web required while bypassing the inertia imposed by the ossified internet infrastructure.

The team's guiding principle was to prioritize user experience above all else. Every millisecond saved in connection setup, every reduction in retransmission delays, and every improvement in throughput would compound across the billions of requests handled by Google's services daily. The first challenge they faced was how to break free from TCP's limitations while maintaining compatibility with the internet's middleboxes. Instead of building an entirely new transport protocol from scratch, which would almost certainly be blocked by firewalls and NATs, the team made the strategic decision to build on top of UDP. UDP's minimal interference from middleboxes provided a flexible canvas, giving engineers the freedom to experiment with congestion control, stream multiplexing, and integrated encryption without the burden of legacy restrictions.

From the outset, Google's prototype of QUIC was bold in its goals. It aimed to fuse transport-layer functionality with security, incorporating TLS directly into the protocol rather than layering it on top as TCP had done for decades. This innovation would reduce the number of round trips needed to establish a secure connection and help eliminate redundant handshake processes. Early experiments showed that by streamlining the handshake, QUIC could deliver significant reductions in latency, particularly in scenarios where connections were repeatedly established and resumed, such as mobile browsing.

The decision to tightly integrate encryption was also reflective of Google's growing commitment to a more secure web. In parallel to the development of QUIC, Google was a vocal proponent of HTTPS adoption, pushing for encrypted connections to become the default standard across the web. QUIC's built-in security model complemented this vision, ensuring that every connection established via QUIC would be encrypted by default, a paradigm shift in transport-layer design.

As Google's engineers iterated on their prototype, they sought to solve not only latency issues but also to address the inefficiencies associated with TCP's head-of-line blocking. This phenomenon, where the loss of a single packet stalls the delivery of all subsequent packets within a stream, had long been a bane for performance-sensitive applications. QUIC's introduction of independent streams within a single connection, each capable of progressing separately despite packet loss in others, provided a breakthrough. In early testing, this approach demonstrated marked improvements for services like Google Search and YouTube, where multiple resources needed to be loaded in parallel to deliver a complete user experience.

To validate the real-world performance of their experimental protocol, Google began deploying early versions of QUIC within its own ecosystem. Chrome, Google's flagship browser, became a crucial testing ground. By silently enabling QUIC for a subset of users, Google could gather invaluable telemetry on how QUIC performed compared to TCP and TLS combinations under various network conditions. This data-driven approach allowed the engineering team to iterate quickly, refining congestion control algorithms, optimizing handshake mechanisms, and adjusting parameters to maximize efficiency.

One of the most remarkable aspects of Google's experimental approach was its scale. Few organizations could deploy a cutting-edge transport protocol to millions of users in a controlled manner, gather telemetry, and iterate based on real-world feedback as rapidly as Google did. This unprecedented level of experimentation and deployment capability was a key factor in QUIC's rapid maturation from an internal project to a viable candidate for standardization.

Despite the promising results, Google's engineers were fully aware that a proprietary transport protocol limited to their own services would ultimately fall short of achieving the broader impact they envisioned. As such, Google took deliberate steps to open up the project, engaging with the broader internet community and the Internet Engineering Task Force (IETF) to transition QUIC from an internal experiment to an open standard. This transition marked a turning point, transforming QUIC from a Google-centric optimization into a collaborative effort to reshape the future of internet transport.

The early experimentation at Google was not without its challenges. Issues related to debugging, interoperability with existing network infrastructure, and fine-tuning congestion control in the wild required continuous attention. However, these hurdles only strengthened the resolve of the engineers behind QUIC, who understood that building a next-generation transport protocol meant confronting and overcoming the complexity of a deeply entrenched internet ecosystem.

Google's experimental beginnings with QUIC exemplify how the drive for performance, security, and innovation can lead to groundbreaking advancements. By daring to rethink transport protocols from first principles and by leveraging their unique scale for real-world validation, Google not only created a faster, more reliable foundation for their services but also set the stage for a broader industry shift. The lessons learned during these formative years would go on to shape the collaborative standardization process that brought QUIC into the mainstream, influencing the evolution of internet transport for years to come.

QUIC vs. TCP: A New Paradigm

The emergence of QUIC marked a decisive shift in how engineers approached internet transport, challenging decades of dominance by TCP. While TCP had been the backbone of reliable internet communication since the late 1970s, QUIC arrived with a fundamentally different design philosophy, addressing long-standing inefficiencies and introducing a fresh set of capabilities tailored for the demands of the modern internet. The comparison between QUIC and TCP reveals not just incremental improvements but a paradigm shift in how connections are established, data is transmitted, and security is enforced across the global network.

At its core, TCP is a transport layer protocol designed to provide reliable, ordered delivery of data over an unreliable IP network. It accomplishes this through mechanisms such as packet retransmission, flow control, and congestion control, all of which have been fine-tuned over decades to work across a wide variety of network conditions. Yet, TCP's strengths are also tied to its constraints. It is tightly coupled with the operating system kernel, making updates or modifications slow and often reliant on widespread adoption of new kernel versions. This inflexibility has been a major contributor to the ossification of TCP, leaving the internet transport ecosystem resistant to innovation at the transport layer.

QUIC, in contrast, is designed as a user-space protocol, freeing it from the constraints of kernel-level implementations. This architectural decision allows for rapid iteration, enabling developers to deploy updates and improvements much faster than is possible with TCP. This agility has given QUIC an edge in adapting to evolving network demands, particularly as modern internet usage has shifted toward mobile-first, real-time, and highly interactive applications.

Perhaps the most visible difference between QUIC and TCP lies in connection establishment. A TCP connection requires a three-way handshake, with an additional round trip if encryption via TLS is desired, resulting in delays before actual data transmission can begin. QUIC collapses these steps by integrating TLS 1.3 directly into its handshake process, allowing encryption and transport handshakes to occur simultaneously. In many scenarios, QUIC enables data to be sent as early as the first round trip, and with connection resumption, it can achieve 0-RTT, sending data immediately with no additional handshake overhead. This reduction in latency is especially impactful in environments with high round-trip times, such as mobile or satellite networks, where every millisecond of delay compounds into a noticeable degradation of user experience.

Another critical area where QUIC departs from TCP is in its handling of multiplexed streams. TCP provides a single ordered byte stream, which becomes a bottleneck under certain conditions. A lost packet within a TCP stream blocks all subsequent packets, even if they belong to unrelated resources. This is the well-known head-of-line blocking issue, which can severely degrade performance for modern web pages that require concurrent loading of multiple assets. While HTTP/2 introduced multiplexing at the application layer, it still relied on TCP underneath, meaning that TCP's head-of-line blocking persisted.

QUIC resolves this problem by offering true transport-level multiplexing. Multiple independent streams coexist within a single QUIC connection, each with its own flow control and packet management. If packet loss occurs on one stream, it does not impede the progress of other streams within the same connection. This approach drastically improves performance in situations where multiple assets are fetched simultaneously, as is common in today's web applications. The ability to mitigate head-of-line blocking at the transport level is one of QUIC's most celebrated achievements, helping to reduce page load times and improve responsiveness across a wide array of services.

Security is another arena where QUIC redefines expectations. While TCP relies on TLS layered above the transport layer for encryption, QUIC bakes encryption into the protocol itself. This not only streamlines connection establishment but also ensures that all QUIC traffic is encrypted by default. By designing encryption as an inseparable part of the protocol, QUIC prevents scenarios where unencrypted fallback mechanisms could be exploited, a concern that has persisted in legacy systems relying on TCP. Moreover, QUIC's encryption of even the transport metadata, such as packet numbers and stream identifiers, helps protect users against passive network observers and limits the information available to potential attackers.

QUIC's ability to support connection migration is another stark departure from TCP's static model. In TCP, connections are tied to the IP addresses and ports of both endpoints, making them brittle in mobile contexts where devices frequently switch between networks or acquire new IP addresses. A change in network environment typically forces a complete teardown and reestablishment of the connection. QUIC, however, is designed to survive such transitions. By using connection identifiers that are independent of IP addresses, QUIC allows active sessions to persist seamlessly across network changes. This capability is a crucial advantage in mobile networks, enabling smoother transitions and reducing interruptions in services such as video calls, live streaming, or real-time gaming.

From a congestion control perspective, both TCP and QUIC share similar foundational algorithms, but QUIC's user-space implementation grants it the flexibility to experiment and iterate much faster. Developers can deploy new congestion control mechanisms tailored to specific applications or network environments without waiting for system-wide updates or changes to kernel-level TCP stacks. This adaptability is vital in an era where network conditions vary widely, from fiber-optic broadband to unstable cellular connections in remote areas.

Despite these advantages, QUIC does face its own challenges. Operating over UDP makes it susceptible to being deprioritized or blocked by certain network devices or middleboxes, which traditionally treat UDP as expendable or insecure. Nonetheless, QUIC was designed with techniques to navigate this ecosystem, such as using encrypted transport parameters and implementing mechanisms like stateless resets to recover from interruptions.

Ultimately, the comparison between QUIC and TCP highlights a broader shift in transport protocol design. TCP was engineered for a simpler, more predictable internet, where static connections and modest data demands were the norm. QUIC, on the other hand, is a product of today's internet, where applications must perform reliably under variable conditions, across mobile networks, and in environments where latency, security, and performance are paramount. The shift from TCP's kernel-bound rigidity to QUIC's user-space flexibility, from unencrypted defaults to mandatory encryption, from single-stream limitations to true multiplexing, illustrates the emergence of a transport paradigm that reflects the realities and aspirations of a modern, dynamic internet.

As more services adopt QUIC and the protocol continues to evolve, it is becoming increasingly evident that QUIC is not merely a replacement for TCP but a reinvention of what transport protocols can and should achieve. It brings to the forefront a philosophy of transport-layer agility, one that aligns with the rapid development cycles and performance expectations of contemporary applications and users worldwide.

UDP as QUIC's Foundation

The decision to build QUIC on top of UDP was a pivotal moment that shaped the entire trajectory of the protocol. It was not an arbitrary choice but a strategic one, rooted in the realities of how the modern internet functions and how entrenched its infrastructure had become.

By the time QUIC was conceived, TCP was firmly embedded in the DNA of the internet. From routers to firewalls to NATs, countless devices and systems were built with assumptions about how TCP behaved. This deeply rooted reliance on TCP presented a formidable challenge for anyone seeking to deploy a transport protocol that was truly new. Instead of attempting to compete directly with TCP at its level, the designers of QUIC decided to sidestep the ossified layers of the internet by leveraging the relative simplicity and flexibility of UDP.

UDP, or User Datagram Protocol, has long existed as a minimalist transport layer protocol. Its defining characteristic is its lack of state and simplicity—it sends datagrams without establishing a connection and does not guarantee delivery, ordering, or protection against duplication. This bare-bones functionality was precisely what made UDP attractive for certain types of applications such as DNS queries, VoIP, and online gaming, where low latency and speed were paramount. However, it also made UDP a prime candidate as a foundation for a more sophisticated transport protocol that could layer its own reliability and congestion control mechanisms on top.

One of the key motivators for using UDP was to bypass the barriers posed by middleboxes. Over the years, the internet had become littered with devices that performed various types of deep packet inspection, traffic shaping, and filtering. Many of these middleboxes were designed with fixed assumptions about TCP, expecting certain handshake patterns, congestion control behaviors, and flow control mechanisms. Introducing a new transport protocol at the same level as TCP would have likely encountered blocks, slow adoption, or unpredictable behavior as middleboxes interfered with or outright rejected unfamiliar traffic. UDP, on the other hand, was less scrutinized by these devices. Because it lacked a handshake and stateful connection semantics, it was generally treated more permissively by middleboxes, making it a flexible platform on which new transport innovations could be deployed.

UDP also offered freedom from the constraints of operating system kernels. Since most TCP stacks are implemented in the kernel, updates and innovations to TCP require kernel-level changes, which are often slow to propagate across diverse systems. By contrast, UDP is exposed to applications through a simple API, giving developers the ability to implement custom behavior in user space. This allows QUIC to evolve independently of operating system releases, enabling faster iteration cycles and experimentation with new features like advanced congestion control algorithms, stream multiplexing, and connection migration.

The simplicity of UDP, however, meant that QUIC had to shoulder the burden of implementing many features typically handled by TCP. This included ensuring reliable delivery, managing packet ordering, detecting packet loss, and implementing sophisticated congestion control. Rather than viewing this as a drawback, QUIC's designers embraced the opportunity to reimagine these mechanisms with modern needs in mind. For example, QUIC was able to avoid TCP's head-of-line blocking issue by supporting multiple independent streams within a single connection, all while managing flow control at the stream level rather than at the connection level.

Another advantage of building on UDP was the flexibility it provided for integrating security directly into the transport protocol. Unlike TCP, which relied on a layered approach where TLS was applied above the transport layer, QUIC natively integrated TLS 1.3 into its handshake process. This meant that QUIC connections could establish secure sessions faster, with fewer round trips than traditional TCP+TLS combinations. UDP's lack of interference in this space gave QUIC the room to craft an entirely new handshake mechanism that combined transport and cryptographic negotiations into a single step, leading to significant reductions in latency, especially in high-latency or mobile networks.

UDP's stateless nature also aligned well with QUIC's ambitions for mobility and connection migration. Traditional TCP connections are bound to specific IP addresses and ports, making them vulnerable to disruptions when network conditions change—such as when a mobile user switches from Wi-Fi to cellular data. With UDP as the foundation, QUIC could build a transport protocol that identified connections not by IP addresses but by opaque connection IDs. These IDs enabled a connection to persist even as the underlying network path changed, offering seamless transitions across networks without requiring a full reconnection, something TCP could not natively provide.

Despite its benefits, building on top of UDP was not without challenges. Because many network administrators treat UDP traffic as less critical or even suspicious, QUIC traffic sometimes faced aggressive throttling, blocking, or prioritization issues, especially in older or more conservative network environments. QUIC's designers addressed these obstacles by incorporating mechanisms like packet padding to disguise traffic patterns and stateless resets to help with graceful recovery when connections were disrupted by middleboxes. These efforts underscored the reality that while UDP provided a powerful foundation, deploying a protocol like QUIC still required careful engineering to navigate the quirks of the existing internet.

By standing on UDP's shoulders, QUIC redefined the role that UDP could play in modern transport. No longer was UDP limited to simple, best-effort datagram delivery. It became the scaffolding for a transport protocol that could match and even surpass TCP in reliability, security, and performance. UDP's openness allowed QUIC to build a comprehensive transport solution complete with congestion control, connection management, flow control, and encryption, all while avoiding many of the legacy pitfalls that TCP had accrued over decades of usage.

The choice to use UDP as QUIC's foundation reflects a pragmatic recognition of how the internet operates today. Rather than attempting to dismantle the deeply ingrained habits of the network stack, QUIC's architects found a path that blended compatibility with innovation. UDP provided a tunnel through which a next-generation protocol could emerge without waiting for a global overhaul of existing infrastructure.

This foundational decision unlocked the ability for QUIC to thrive where TCP struggled: in mobile networks, in real-time applications, in environments where agility and low latency were paramount. By leveraging UDP, QUIC not only bypassed the ossification of the transport layer but also offered a glimpse into a future where innovation could continue above legacy protocols without being stifled by them. The marriage of UDP's flexibility with QUIC's cutting-edge transport features marked the beginning of a new era for internet communications, setting the stage for the protocol's rapid adoption and its evolution into a new internet standard.

Handshake Innovation: Faster Connections

One of the most significant breakthroughs that QUIC introduced to the world of internet transport was its reimagination of the handshake process. The handshake, the sequence of steps that two endpoints perform to establish a secure and reliable connection, has always been a critical component of how data is exchanged on the internet. For decades, the handshake mechanisms in TCP and TLS formed the backbone of secure online communications. However, while these traditional methods have been effective at establishing connections, they have also introduced unavoidable latency, especially over networks with high round-trip times. QUIC fundamentally changed this narrative by merging and streamlining the handshake process, making faster connections not just a goal but a built-in feature.

In the TCP model, establishing a secure connection typically involves two distinct stages. First, there is the TCP three-way handshake, where the client and server exchange SYN, SYN-ACK, and ACK packets to initiate the connection. Once the TCP handshake is complete, a separate handshake is required for the TLS layer to negotiate encryption parameters and verify identities. This process, in total, often requires two round trips between the client and server before any application data can be securely transmitted. In environments with stable and low-latency networks, these handshakes may seem negligible. However, in mobile networks, satellite connections, or regions with poor connectivity, the accumulated delay can have a significant negative impact on user experience.

QUIC approached this problem by collapsing the transport and cryptographic handshakes into a single process. From its inception, QUIC was designed to integrate TLS 1.3 directly into its handshake, eliminating the need for sequential, layered negotiations. By embedding the cryptographic handshake within the transport handshake, QUIC allowed connections to be established in just one round trip under normal conditions, and even zero round trips when session resumption is possible. This innovative design has had profound implications for reducing latency and improving the responsiveness of modern web applications.

28

The key to QUIC's faster handshake lies in its use of pre-shared cryptographic information and connection identifiers. When a client connects to a server for the first time, it completes a 1-RTT handshake, during which it receives a set of cryptographic parameters and tokens that can be reused for future connections. These tokens allow the client to attempt a 0-RTT handshake in subsequent sessions with the same server, enabling it to send encrypted application data immediately without waiting for the full handshake to complete. This capability dramatically improves performance in scenarios where clients frequently reconnect to the same servers, such as with content delivery networks, streaming platforms, and cloud applications.

In contrast to TCP, where the client and server must exchange several packets before any encrypted data can flow, QUIC's 0-RTT data transmission can significantly reduce the perceived load times for repeat users. This reduction in latency is particularly beneficial in mobile environments, where network conditions may fluctuate and round-trip times can be unpredictable. By enabling immediate data transmission, QUIC enhances user experience, keeping services responsive even when network quality is suboptimal.

Another critical aspect of QUIC's handshake innovation is its resilience to network changes. In the traditional TCP+TLS model, a change in the underlying network path, such as when a mobile user switches from Wi-Fi to cellular data, often results in the need to re-establish the entire connection from scratch. This means repeating both the TCP and TLS handshakes, introducing additional round trips and further delays. QUIC, however, employs connection IDs that are independent of the client's IP address and port, allowing an active connection to persist even if the network path changes. The handshake does not need to be repeated, and the session can continue uninterrupted, providing a seamless experience for users moving across different networks.

Security has always been a critical concern when optimizing handshake performance. QUIC's handshake does not sacrifice security for speed; instead, it strengthens it. By requiring TLS 1.3 as part of its design, QUIC ensures that every connection benefits from forward secrecy, strong encryption, and mutual authentication mechanisms. Moreover, QUIC encrypts most of its own transport headers, preventing attackers and passive observers from gathering metadata that could be exploited for traffic analysis or surveillance. This level of protection was previously unattainable without incurring additional latency when using TCP.

The handshake improvements introduced by QUIC also open new doors for application performance beyond just traditional web browsing. Real-time applications like video conferencing, online gaming, and remote collaboration tools often suffer from the delays caused by traditional handshakes. By drastically reducing the time it takes to establish a secure connection, QUIC enables these applications to deliver more immediate interactions, improving quality of service and user satisfaction.

Another subtle but important benefit of QUIC's handshake model is its efficiency in managing retransmissions. Because QUIC is built on top of UDP and operates in user space, it can recover from lost handshake packets without relying on slower kernel-level retransmission mechanisms. This accelerates the recovery process in lossy networks and prevents handshake delays from ballooning in challenging network conditions.

In deploying QUIC at scale, companies like Google observed significant improvements in connection times across their services. When QUIC was enabled for users of Chrome and YouTube, data showed that connection establishment latency dropped considerably, especially for users on mobile networks and in regions with higher latency. This empirical success validated the handshake innovations at the heart of QUIC and contributed to its momentum as a candidate for industry-wide adoption.

The handshake model introduced by QUIC not only represents an engineering achievement but also reflects a philosophical shift in how transport protocols should function in a modern, mobile-first world. By unifying security and transport layers and focusing on minimizing the time to first byte, QUIC redefines the standard for what users should expect from internet performance. The blend of faster handshakes, seamless connection migration, and robust encryption lays the foundation for a new generation of internet applications where responsiveness and security coexist without compromise.

The handshake innovations of QUIC highlight the power of rethinking long-standing protocols from first principles. By doing so, QUIC has set new expectations for speed and efficiency, shaping the future of how devices communicate securely and swiftly across an ever-expanding global network.

Multiplexing Without Head-of-Line Blocking

One of the most critical innovations that QUIC brought to internet transport is its ability to multiplex streams without suffering from the head-of-line blocking problem that has long plagued TCP-based communications. The concept of multiplexing—the simultaneous transmission of multiple independent streams over a single connection—is not new. However, the way QUIC implements this mechanism represents a fundamental improvement over previous transport protocols, reshaping how applications interact with the network and significantly enhancing the efficiency of data transmission.

In the traditional model, TCP operates as a single ordered byte stream, where all data must arrive in sequence. If a packet is lost in transit, the receiver must wait for that specific packet to be retransmitted and successfully received before it can process any subsequent packets. This phenomenon, known as head-of-line blocking, means that even if later packets have arrived and are sitting ready to be processed, they remain locked behind the missing packet, creating unnecessary latency. This issue became increasingly pronounced as web pages and applications began demanding more and more resources simultaneously. The widespread adoption of HTTP/2 introduced application-layer multiplexing, allowing multiple streams over one TCP connection. Yet, because HTTP/2 still depended on TCP underneath, it could not escape TCP's inherent head-of-line blocking at the transport level.

QUIC approached this challenge with a fresh design, decoupling the transport of individual streams. Instead of a single ordered byte stream

31

like TCP, QUIC allows for multiple concurrent streams to exist within one connection. Each stream is independent, meaning data packets for one stream are unaffected by packet loss or delays occurring on another stream. When packet loss happens within a QUIC connection, only the data associated with the affected stream is delayed, while other streams can continue to deliver data to the application without interruption. This eliminates the cascading delays introduced by head-of-line blocking and provides a substantial improvement in performance for modern web applications.

The advantage of this design is especially evident in scenarios where clients must request numerous assets simultaneously, such as when loading a web page with dozens or hundreds of images, scripts, and style sheets. Under TCP and HTTP/2, a lost packet in the underlying TCP connection could stall the delivery of all other streams sharing that connection, forcing the browser to wait until the retransmission process completed. In contrast, QUIC's architecture allows browsers to continue processing streams whose packets have arrived, ensuring that page rendering can progress smoothly, even while retransmissions are occurring on other streams.

This model also benefits real-time applications. For instance, in video conferencing or online gaming, timely delivery of data is critical to maintaining a fluid and responsive user experience. TCP's head-of-line blocking can introduce noticeable stutters or lag spikes when packet loss occurs, detracting from the quality of the experience. QUIC's ability to isolate streams means that control messages, audio, video, and other data types can be transmitted simultaneously without interfering with one another. A dropped video packet will not delay the reception of critical control data, allowing the application to remain responsive even in suboptimal network conditions.

Under the hood, QUIC achieves this functionality by structuring each stream as a separate flow of data within the same encrypted connection. Each stream maintains its own flow control and sequencing mechanisms, tracked independently by both endpoints. Streams are multiplexed within QUIC packets using lightweight framing, which indicates to the receiver which stream a particular segment of data belongs to. This framing approach, combined with QUIC's use of packet numbers instead of TCP-style sequence numbers, enables highly granular control over which streams are affected by loss and which are free to proceed unhindered.

Another subtle but impactful benefit of QUIC's multiplexing is its efficiency in resource utilization. Because multiple streams share the same connection state, encryption context, and congestion control, QUIC reduces the overhead associated with managing separate connections for each resource, as would be required when using multiple TCP connections. This consolidation reduces CPU and memory consumption on both the client and server sides, contributing to faster performance and improved scalability, especially in environments where thousands of simultaneous streams may be opened by a single client, such as modern browsers interacting with complex web applications.

Additionally, QUIC's multiplexing is well-suited to the shifting landscape of application development, where microservices architectures, serverless computing, and distributed systems are becoming the norm. These paradigms often require frequent and concurrent communication between services. The ability to multiplex streams efficiently and without head-of-line blocking allows services to communicate more fluidly, improving responsiveness and reducing latencies across interconnected systems.

The user-space implementation of QUIC further empowers developers to experiment with stream prioritization, enabling fine-tuned control over which streams should be delivered first. For example, a browser could prioritize HTML and CSS streams to ensure a page's structure and styling load immediately, while delaying lower-priority assets such as background images or deferred JavaScript. This degree of control is difficult to achieve with TCP-based protocols due to the constraints imposed by the transport layer's head-of-line blocking behavior.

The removal of head-of-line blocking at the transport layer also opens new possibilities for handling packet loss and network variability. In QUIC, congestion control and retransmissions are handled at the packet level rather than being tied to a single continuous byte stream. This allows QUIC to recover more gracefully from packet loss and to resume stream data delivery faster than TCP. As network environments become more unpredictable—due to wireless interference, mobile handoffs, or fluctuating bandwidth—QUIC's resilience becomes increasingly valuable.

Importantly, QUIC's multiplexing model also enhances reliability from the perspective of user experience. Users often perceive reliability not just as whether a connection succeeds but as whether their interactions with an application feel smooth and uninterrupted. By ensuring that a hiccup affecting one stream does not ripple through the entire session, QUIC helps maintain consistent interactivity and responsiveness. This smoothness is critical in applications like cloud-based IDEs, collaborative document editors, and remote desktops, where latency spikes or freezes can break workflow continuity.

The shift away from head-of-line blocking is more than a technical milestone; it is a redefinition of how applications and networks interact. By liberating streams from the constraints of a monolithic transport channel, QUIC reflects a design philosophy that prioritizes flexibility, responsiveness, and user-centric performance. It demonstrates that addressing foundational inefficiencies at the transport layer can yield transformative benefits for a wide spectrum of internet applications, from browsing and streaming to gaming and enterprise cloud services.

Multiplexing without head-of-line blocking is one of the reasons QUIC has been so rapidly adopted by major players in the tech industry. As developers and network architects increasingly design with mobile users, distributed systems, and real-time interactions in mind, the need for this kind of transport-level resilience has never been more apparent. QUIC's solution to this long-standing problem exemplifies how reimagining fundamental aspects of internet infrastructure can unlock new levels of efficiency, performance, and reliability.

Encryption by Default

One of the most radical and impactful aspects of QUIC is its decision to enforce encryption as a mandatory, foundational feature of the protocol. Unlike TCP, which was designed in an era when the internet was a cooperative space with few security threats, QUIC was conceived in a digital landscape where privacy and security have become paramount. The modern internet is fraught with dangers: surveillance, data breaches, man-in-the-middle attacks, and sophisticated threat actors targeting individuals, businesses, and entire nations. In this context, encryption can no longer be considered optional or an add-on to transport protocols. QUIC embodies this shift by making encryption an inseparable part of its architecture, thereby establishing encryption by default as a core principle of its design.

Historically, protocols like TCP left security concerns to higher layers of the stack. When the need for confidentiality and authentication arose, solutions like SSL and later TLS were developed to sit on top of TCP, providing encryption for sensitive applications such as online banking, e-commerce, and secure communications. While TLS has been a critical success in securing the web, its implementation as a separate layer introduced friction in terms of latency and deployment. Worse, many applications still operated without encryption for years, exposing users to various risks. Even today, despite widespread adoption of HTTPS, there remain instances where unencrypted connections persist, either due to legacy systems, misconfigurations, or cost concerns.

QUIC eliminates these inconsistencies by integrating TLS 1.3 directly into the transport protocol itself. Every QUIC connection is, by design, encrypted. There is no fallback to an unencrypted mode, and there is no option to transmit data in plaintext. From the very first packet, QUIC encrypts both application data and critical parts of the transport layer, including stream identifiers, acknowledgments, and packet numbers. This level of default protection goes beyond simply securing the content of communications; it shields metadata that could otherwise be exploited for traffic analysis, fingerprinting, or surveillance.

The integration of TLS 1.3 within QUIC not only enhances security but also streamlines performance. In traditional TCP+TLS stacks, a full TLS handshake is layered on top of the three-way TCP handshake, requiring additional round trips before encrypted data can be exchanged. QUIC's merged handshake process allows both the transport and encryption handshakes to occur simultaneously, reducing the number of round trips required to establish a secure session. This improvement is particularly beneficial in high-latency environments, such as mobile networks or geographically distant endpoints, where round-trip delays can degrade user experience.

Encryption by default in QUIC also modernizes the security guarantees provided by transport protocols. While TCP itself offers no protection against tampering or eavesdropping, QUIC ensures confidentiality, integrity, and authenticity for all transmitted data as part of its base functionality. TLS 1.3 further strengthens these guarantees by mandating forward secrecy, ensuring that even if encryption keys are compromised in the future, past communications remain secure. This proactive security stance aligns with the increasing demand for privacy protections from both users and regulatory bodies worldwide.

QUIC's encryption model goes a step further by protecting not only the data payload but also sensitive control information in the packet headers. In traditional TCP traffic, critical metadata such as sequence numbers, window sizes, and acknowledgment numbers are sent in cleartext, making them accessible to anyone observing the network path. While this information is essential for TCP's functionality, it also provides attackers and surveillance systems with valuable insights into connection behavior, such as flow characteristics, application type, or even the specific implementation of the TCP stack being used. QUIC mitigates this risk by encrypting most of its transport metadata, making passive traffic analysis significantly more difficult and increasing users' privacy.

Moreover, QUIC's mandatory encryption has important implications for defending against certain classes of active attacks. For example, it prevents man-in-the-middle attackers from injecting malicious data into the connection or manipulating transport-level behavior such as flow control or stream prioritization. By ensuring that both application data and control signals are encrypted and authenticated, QUIC safeguards against a wide range of attacks that could compromise the integrity and availability of modern applications.

From a deployment perspective, the choice to make encryption non-negotiable simplifies decision-making for developers and organizations. In the TCP world, developers had to choose whether to implement TLS and weigh the trade-offs between performance, complexity, and security. With QUIC, the decision is made upfront—security is always on. This removes a historical barrier that prevented some organizations from fully adopting encrypted communications, whether due to concerns about legacy compatibility or perceived overhead.

The enforcement of encryption by default also reflects broader cultural and regulatory shifts. In recent years, there has been mounting pressure from governments, advocacy groups, and consumers for stronger privacy protections. Laws such as the General Data Protection Regulation (GDPR) in Europe and the California Consumer Privacy Act (CCPA) in the United States have codified the need to protect users' personal data in transit. By mandating encryption at the transport level, QUIC helps organizations meet these legal obligations more easily, reducing the compliance burden and enhancing user trust.

Another often overlooked benefit of QUIC's encryption-first design is its ability to future-proof communications against emerging threats. As quantum computing looms on the horizon and adversaries become more sophisticated, transport protocols must be designed with the agility to adapt to new cryptographic standards and security challenges. By operating in user space and decoupling from the operating system's kernel, QUIC provides the flexibility to incorporate future versions of TLS or even post-quantum cryptographic algorithms without requiring a massive overhaul of the underlying network infrastructure.

Despite the significant advantages, encryption by default does introduce new considerations for network operators. For example, the fact that QUIC encrypts most transport-layer metadata limits the visibility that traditional network monitoring tools have into QUIC traffic. This makes it more challenging to perform functions such as traffic shaping, intrusion detection, and performance analysis using conventional methods. However, this trade-off reflects a growing consensus in the internet community: user privacy and security must take precedence, even if it means rethinking how networks are managed and monitored.

QUIC's mandatory encryption marks a profound shift in how internet transport protocols are designed and deployed. It moves the needle from a world where security was bolted on as an afterthought to one where security is intrinsic to the very fabric of communication. By embedding encryption as a default requirement, QUIC not only protects users and applications but also signals a broader evolution in the priorities of internet engineering—where speed, security, and privacy are no longer mutually exclusive but harmonized within a single, modern protocol.

TLS 1.3 and QUIC: A Perfect Match

The integration of TLS 1.3 into QUIC represents one of the most important milestones in the evolution of secure and efficient internet communications. While QUIC introduces a host of transport-layer innovations, its true power is realized through its symbiotic relationship with TLS 1.3. The marriage of these two technologies solves long-standing issues in latency, security, and flexibility that have challenged internet protocols for decades. Together, they form a powerful and forward-looking combination that redefines how modern applications achieve both speed and robust encryption.

TLS, or Transport Layer Security, has been the gold standard for securing data in transit over the internet. For years, TLS evolved to address emerging threats and vulnerabilities, but it was often constrained by its relationship with TCP. Traditionally, TLS was implemented as a layer above TCP, providing the necessary cryptographic handshake and protection for application data. While effective, this layered approach introduced performance bottlenecks. Before any encrypted data could be sent, a TCP connection had to be fully established via a three-way handshake, followed by a separate multi-step TLS handshake. Each of these stages required additional round trips between client and server, introducing latency that became increasingly problematic as the internet shifted toward mobile-first and real-time applications.

The arrival of TLS 1.3 marked a substantial leap forward in addressing these inefficiencies. TLS 1.3 reduced the number of handshake messages required to establish a secure connection compared to its predecessors. It also eliminated outdated cryptographic algorithms, streamlined session establishment, and offered forward secrecy as a default feature. By minimizing handshake complexity and enhancing security, TLS 1.3 set the stage for tighter integration with emerging transport protocols.

QUIC took full advantage of these improvements by embedding TLS 1.3 directly within the transport layer. This decision was both strategic and practical. QUIC's architects recognized that integrating encryption and transport functionality into a single handshake could drastically reduce connection establishment times while preserving, and even enhancing, security guarantees. By tightly coupling QUIC with TLS 1.3, they created a protocol that could accomplish what had long seemed mutually exclusive: fast, low-latency connections that are secure by default.

One of the most significant benefits of this integration is the reduction in round-trip time. With TLS 1.3 built directly into QUIC's handshake, a new connection can be securely established in just one round trip, rather than the two or more required by traditional TCP+TLS stacks. In scenarios where session resumption is possible, QUIC and TLS 1.3 enable zero-round-trip time (0-RTT) handshakes, allowing encrypted application data to be sent with the very first packet. This acceleration is critical in today's internet landscape, where mobile networks with fluctuating latency and variable reliability are commonplace.

The synergy between TLS 1.3 and QUIC also improves connection robustness. In legacy protocols, switching between networks—such as moving from Wi-Fi to a cellular connection—would typically break the TCP connection, forcing both the transport and TLS handshakes to be re-initiated. With QUIC, which employs connection IDs that are independent of IP addresses and ports, sessions can persist across network changes without requiring a new TLS handshake. This results in a seamless experience for users, whether they are watching a video on a mobile device while walking between Wi-Fi hotspots or engaging in a video call as their connection switches to cellular data.

Another major advantage of combining TLS 1.3 with QUIC is the expanded encryption coverage. In traditional TCP+TLS models, only the application layer data (for example, HTTP requests and responses) is encrypted, while transport-level metadata like sequence numbers, acknowledgment numbers, and flow control signals remain exposed. QUIC, leveraging TLS 1.3's cryptographic framework, encrypts not only the application data but also much of its transport-layer metadata. This protects against passive traffic analysis and fingerprinting attacks that have historically been a weakness in protocols like TCP.

The handshake process itself in QUIC is also more efficient and adaptable thanks to TLS 1.3. During a QUIC handshake, the TLS handshake occurs inside QUIC's transport handshake, leveraging QUIC packets to exchange the necessary TLS handshake messages. This approach removes redundant messaging and eliminates the need to coordinate separate transport and security layers. As a result, connection setup is not only faster but also simpler from an engineering perspective, reducing overhead and improving consistency across different applications.

TLS 1.3's adoption of modern cryptographic primitives further strengthens QUIC's security posture. Support for outdated and vulnerable algorithms, such as RC4 and MD5, was removed from TLS 1.3, ensuring that all QUIC connections are protected by state-of-the-art encryption methods like AEAD (Authenticated Encryption with Associated Data) ciphers. This guarantees both confidentiality and integrity for each QUIC packet, mitigating risks associated with tampering, replay attacks, and unauthorized data disclosure.

Performance is further enhanced by TLS 1.3's built-in support for 0-RTT early data, which QUIC uses to send encrypted application data immediately after the initial handshake message, under specific conditions. This feature is particularly useful for connections to services that clients frequently revisit, such as major content delivery networks or popular web platforms. However, QUIC also incorporates safeguards to mitigate the replay attack risks associated with 0-RTT data, such as limiting the types of operations permitted during early data exchanges and tying tokens to client IP addresses or other identifiers.

The combination of QUIC and TLS 1.3 also introduces operational benefits. For developers and system administrators, the integration simplifies the deployment process. There is no longer a need to separately configure and manage TLS and transport-layer settings;

encryption is inherently part of the transport mechanism. This consolidation streamlines configuration and reduces the likelihood of misconfigurations that could expose applications to vulnerabilities.

Additionally, the modularity of QUIC and TLS 1.3 enables future-proofing. As new versions of TLS emerge or as cryptographic best practices evolve—such as the potential need to implement post-quantum cryptography—QUIC's user-space implementation allows developers to update TLS libraries and protocols independently of the operating system's kernel. This capability accelerates the adoption of stronger cryptographic protections without waiting for OS-level support or widespread infrastructure changes.

TLS 1.3 and QUIC together reflect a paradigm shift in protocol design. They represent a unified vision where security and performance are no longer competing priorities but are instead complementary elements. By deeply integrating encryption into the transport layer, QUIC and TLS 1.3 offer users an internet experience that is faster, more secure, and more adaptable to modern usage patterns.

The success of QUIC's and TLS 1.3's integration has also influenced other areas of protocol development and deployment. As browsers, cloud providers, and content delivery networks increasingly adopt QUIC, they are raising the baseline for secure and efficient communications across the web. The joint power of TLS 1.3 and QUIC has enabled services like YouTube, Google Search, and many others to deliver faster, more secure connections to users worldwide, demonstrating the real-world impact of marrying these two modern protocols.

The perfect match between TLS 1.3 and QUIC is not merely a technical improvement; it is a reflection of the evolving priorities of the internet community. It recognizes that security should not come at the expense of speed and that performance should never undermine privacy. By solving these challenges together, TLS 1.3 and QUIC set a new standard for what secure and efficient communications should look like in the modern internet age.

Early Adoption in Chrome

The story of QUIC's early adoption is inextricably linked to Google Chrome, the world's most widely used web browser. As Google was both the creator of QUIC and the developer of Chrome, it had a unique advantage in testing and deploying this next-generation transport protocol directly to millions of users. Chrome became the natural proving ground for QUIC, providing Google with an unparalleled platform to validate its new protocol under real-world conditions and at a massive scale. This early adoption phase was crucial not just for gathering performance data, but for shaping QUIC into a protocol ready for the wider internet.

Chrome, already commanding a large market share in the browser space, was an ideal vehicle to experiment with QUIC outside of lab environments. By integrating QUIC directly into Chrome's networking stack, Google could selectively enable the protocol for certain users or specific domains. This incremental rollout strategy allowed engineers to monitor QUIC's behavior under a wide variety of network conditions, devices, and geographic locations. Chrome users became the first participants in one of the largest controlled experiments ever conducted on transport-layer optimization.

One of the earliest testbeds for QUIC inside Chrome was Google Search. Given the global scale of search traffic and its sensitivity to latency, this service provided immediate and meaningful insights into how QUIC could enhance user experience. Google quickly observed that users connecting to its servers via QUIC experienced consistently faster page loads compared to those using traditional TCP with TLS. These results were particularly striking for users on mobile networks, where the combination of QUIC's reduced handshake latency and its resilience to packet loss helped counteract the inherent challenges of cellular connectivity.

YouTube soon followed as another major service enabled for QUIC within Chrome. Video streaming presented a different but equally valuable use case. Video buffering and startup times are key performance indicators for streaming services, directly influencing user engagement and satisfaction. Google's telemetry revealed that QUIC could reduce video start times and lower the frequency of playback interruptions, thanks to its ability to multiplex streams and handle packet loss more gracefully than TCP. With these performance gains, Google was able to deliver smoother video experiences to Chrome users without requiring changes on the end-user's part.

Chrome's early adoption of QUIC also exposed important challenges that would help refine the protocol. One such challenge involved middlebox interference. While building QUIC on top of UDP allowed it to bypass many of the limitations imposed by TCP ossification, it also meant encountering networks that treated UDP traffic as second-class or even blocked it outright. Chrome's vast user base gave Google the data it needed to identify these problematic networks. In response, Chrome was engineered to gracefully fall back to traditional TCP+TLS when QUIC could not be established. This fallback mechanism was essential to ensuring that user experience was never degraded, even on networks hostile to UDP.

In addition to performance monitoring, Chrome's early deployment of QUIC allowed Google to study the behavior of QUIC's novel congestion control algorithms under diverse conditions. With so many users generating real traffic, Google was able to test and refine its implementation of congestion control mechanisms such as BBR (Bottleneck Bandwidth and Round-trip propagation time), which aimed to better utilize available bandwidth while minimizing packet loss and latency. Chrome's feedback loop provided real-world data that would have been impossible to fully replicate in controlled lab environments, allowing QUIC to evolve rapidly in response to actual usage patterns.

Chrome also played a critical role in educating developers and the wider internet community about the potential of QUIC. As more developers became aware that Chrome users were silently benefiting from a faster transport protocol, interest in QUIC outside of Google grew. Discussions began to emerge around standardization and the broader applicability of QUIC beyond Google's services. Chrome's role in this process was foundational, serving as both an experimental platform and a showcase for QUIC's advantages.

The early adoption of QUIC in Chrome also highlighted the importance of developer tooling and diagnostics. To support engineers in diagnosing issues and optimizing QUIC connections, Google enhanced Chrome's developer tools to include visibility into whether QUIC was being used and how connections were performing. This transparency not only empowered developers to experiment with and fine-tune their own applications but also fostered a growing awareness of how transport-layer decisions could directly impact user experience.

During this early phase, Google maintained a careful balance between experimentation and production readiness. Chrome's team gradually expanded QUIC's reach, initially enabling it only for Google-owned services before cautiously allowing other domains to experiment. Chrome's telemetry provided Google with deep insights into metrics such as connection success rates, error rates, latency, and bandwidth utilization, enabling them to iterate on QUIC's design in response to findings from live deployments.

The success of QUIC within Chrome eventually became impossible to ignore. Not only did Google validate that QUIC improved page load times, video playback, and resilience on unreliable networks, but it also proved that deploying a major transport protocol update was feasible in today's complex internet ecosystem. Chrome demonstrated that even with middleboxes, firewalls, and a wide array of end-user devices, QUIC could operate effectively and deliver measurable benefits.

As Chrome users reaped the rewards of these behind-the-scenes improvements, Google continued to push for QUIC's broader adoption, submitting the protocol to the IETF for standardization. The positive results from Chrome's early adoption played a significant role in convincing other stakeholders in the internet community that QUIC was not just a niche experiment but a viable successor to TCP.

Chrome's early deployment of QUIC set a precedent for how future internet protocols could be developed and deployed. By leveraging its massive user base, Google was able to move beyond theory and simulations to gather data from real-world usage at an unprecedented scale. The lessons learned from Chrome's early adoption phase helped shape QUIC into a protocol ready for global deployment, influencing not just the trajectory of QUIC itself, but also how other large-scale engineering projects might approach transport-layer innovation in the years ahead.

The partnership between Chrome and QUIC remains one of the clearest examples of how tight integration between software platforms and protocol development can accelerate technological progress. By embedding QUIC within Chrome's networking stack, Google created a feedback loop between users and protocol designers that enabled rapid iteration, real-world validation, and ultimately a transport protocol poised to become a new standard for the modern web.

HTTP/3: QUIC Takes the Stage

The arrival of HTTP/3 marked a pivotal moment in the evolution of internet protocols, a moment where QUIC's innovations moved from experimental to mainstream. For years, the internet's most common protocol for transferring web pages, HTTP, was tightly coupled with TCP. HTTP/1.1 and even HTTP/2, despite introducing multiplexing at the application layer, still relied on TCP underneath. This dependency carried forward all the limitations of TCP, including head-of-line blocking at the transport layer, sluggish connection setup due to multiple round trips, and constrained flexibility in adapting to modern network conditions. HTTP/3 changed this by becoming the first version of HTTP to be built directly on top of QUIC, ushering in a new era of faster, more efficient, and more secure web communication.

The decision to base HTTP/3 on QUIC was not made lightly. The internet had long suffered from the legacy limitations imposed by TCP's architecture. While HTTP/2 attempted to address some performance bottlenecks through multiplexing and header compression, it could not escape the fundamental nature of TCP's ordered byte stream. If a single TCP packet was lost, every multiplexed stream running over that connection would stall, leading to delays in delivering all in-flight resources. For modern web applications, which often require loading dozens or even hundreds of assets in parallel, this inefficiency became a growing concern, especially on lossy or high-latency networks like mobile or satellite links.

QUIC offered a way out of this dilemma. By supporting true transport-level multiplexing without head-of-line blocking, QUIC provided the foundation for HTTP/3 to fully realize the performance improvements that HTTP/2 had only partially achieved. HTTP/3 built on QUIC's native streams, allowing each HTTP request and response pair to operate independently. This meant that if one packet belonging to a single HTTP stream was lost, it would no longer block unrelated streams from progressing. The result was a dramatic reduction in page load times and an overall smoother experience for end users, particularly in conditions where packet loss was common.

One of the defining characteristics of HTTP/3 is how it reduces latency during connection establishment. Because QUIC integrates TLS 1.3 into its handshake process, HTTP/3 connections benefit from faster session setups. A traditional HTTP/2 connection over TCP and TLS might require two or more round trips before data could begin flowing. HTTP/3, by contrast, can start sending encrypted application data in a single round trip, or even immediately in the case of resumed connections using 0-RTT. This improvement is not just theoretical. In production environments, organizations deploying HTTP/3 consistently observed faster initial page loads and reduced time to first byte, leading to better performance metrics and a more responsive web.

Security is another domain where HTTP/3, through QUIC, took a firm stance. Previous versions of HTTP could technically operate over plaintext TCP connections, though the widespread push for HTTPS and TLS helped mitigate this vulnerability over time. HTTP/3 enforces encryption by design, as QUIC itself mandates the use of TLS 1.3. Every HTTP/3 connection is encrypted from the outset, eliminating the possibility of unencrypted fallback and guaranteeing that every request and response is protected from eavesdropping, tampering, and man-in-the-middle attacks. This baked-in security aligns HTTP/3 with modern expectations of privacy and integrity, contributing to a safer internet ecosystem.

HTTP/3's debut also coincided with the growing dominance of mobile and wireless networks, which posed unique challenges to older transport models. Mobile users frequently switch between networks—jumping from Wi-Fi to cellular data, for instance—which historically broke TCP connections and forced expensive reconnects. With QUIC's use of connection IDs instead of relying on IP addresses, HTTP/3 can maintain active sessions even as the underlying network path changes.

This connection migration capability is crucial in delivering seamless experiences to users who move between networks while watching videos, gaming, or using cloud applications.

Another noteworthy advantage of HTTP/3 is its improved handling of congestion control and packet recovery. TCP, constrained by kernel-space implementations and legacy middlebox interference, has seen slow evolution in congestion algorithms. QUIC, operating in user space, allows HTTP/3 to take advantage of modern congestion control schemes like Google's BBR, which is designed to better utilize available bandwidth while avoiding unnecessary packet drops. Additionally, QUIC's packet-level retransmission strategies are more granular than TCP's stream-based recovery, further enhancing the resilience and speed of HTTP/3 connections.

The early deployments of HTTP/3 were driven by major players like Google, Facebook, and Cloudflare, who quickly realized the potential of QUIC-powered HTTP in their large-scale infrastructure. These organizations began enabling HTTP/3 support on their services, which led to significant real-world performance improvements for end users. At the same time, browser vendors such as Google (with Chrome) and Mozilla (with Firefox) introduced early support for HTTP/3, allowing the protocol to gain traction among millions of users almost overnight.

HTTP/3's rollout highlighted another key aspect of its adoption story—the role of Content Delivery Networks (CDNs). CDNs, which cache and serve content closer to end users to reduce latency, were among the first to recognize the value of HTTP/3. By deploying HTTP/3 at the edge of their networks, CDNs enabled faster and more reliable content delivery for geographically distributed users. The benefits were especially noticeable for mobile users in regions with less reliable infrastructure, where the advantages of QUIC's reduced handshake overhead and stream independence were most impactful.

The adoption of HTTP/3 also prompted discussions across the internet community about monitoring and managing traffic. With QUIC encrypting not just the payload but also much of the transport metadata, traditional network monitoring tools faced challenges in analyzing traffic flows. Yet, the consensus was clear: the trade-off between visibility and security favored end-user protection and data confidentiality. As a result, new tools and methods were developed to provide operators with insights into HTTP/3 performance while respecting the protocol's enhanced privacy features.

As HTTP/3 took the stage, it signified more than just a technical upgrade; it represented a shift in how the web itself is expected to perform. The protocol embodies the lessons learned from HTTP/1.1 and HTTP/2 while taking full advantage of QUIC's revolutionary transport model. It also symbolizes the broader trend in internet engineering, where speed, resilience, and security are increasingly treated as inseparable pillars of modern web communication.

The transition to HTTP/3 has not been without challenges. Support for HTTP/3 in legacy devices and networks varies, and middlebox interference with UDP traffic can still occasionally disrupt QUIC-based connections. However, fallback mechanisms ensure that when HTTP/3 cannot be used, clients can seamlessly revert to HTTP/2 or HTTP/1.1 over TCP. Meanwhile, continuous improvements in network infrastructure and the increasing prevalence of QUIC-friendly middleboxes are steadily smoothing the path for HTTP/3's wider adoption.

HTTP/3's integration with QUIC ultimately signifies a bold rethinking of the internet's foundational protocols. By addressing fundamental flaws in earlier transport layers and aligning itself with the security and performance needs of a rapidly evolving web, HTTP/3 has become a cornerstone of the next-generation internet experience. Its widespread deployment promises a faster, safer, and more resilient online world for billions of users around the globe.

Transport Layer Reimagined

The creation of QUIC signified a radical shift in how the transport layer of the internet is conceived, designed, and deployed. For decades, the transport layer was seen through the lens of TCP and UDP, two stalwart protocols that formed the backbone of global communications. TCP provided reliability and ordering, while UDP offered speed and simplicity. However, both were products of an earlier internet, designed in a time when the network was largely academic, the number of users was comparatively small, and security was often an afterthought. The modern internet, defined by mobile devices, streaming services, cloud applications, and persistent security threats, demanded more. The arrival of QUIC was not merely an upgrade to these protocols, but a reimagination of the transport layer itself.

At the heart of this reimagination is the concept that transport should no longer be rigid, inflexible, or hampered by decades of infrastructure ossification. QUIC challenged this norm by decoupling itself from the kernel and operating entirely in user space. This change alone was revolutionary. While TCP implementations are typically baked into operating system kernels and require coordinated system-wide updates to evolve, QUIC's user-space design allows developers to iterate rapidly. Applications can bundle their own QUIC implementations, enabling new features and optimizations to be delivered directly with application updates, bypassing the slow-moving machinery of OS releases.

The shift to user space also opened the door to a more modular and adaptable protocol. In QUIC, the components that traditionally defined the transport layer—handshake, congestion control, stream management, and packet retransmission—are no longer monolithic and static. Each of these elements is now flexible and extensible, designed to be adjusted or replaced based on evolving needs. This modularity reflects the changing nature of internet applications. From video conferencing to cloud gaming, from distributed databases to IoT systems, modern applications have diverse and sometimes conflicting demands on transport protocols. QUIC, by design, allows applications to adapt its mechanisms to specific use cases without disrupting other parts of the protocol.

QUIC also challenged the longstanding paradigm of separating transport from security. Historically, transport protocols like TCP handled connection establishment and reliability, while security was layered on top via protocols like TLS. This model, while functional, introduced inefficiencies, particularly in the form of redundant handshakes and increased latency. QUIC reimagined this relationship by integrating TLS 1.3 directly into its core, treating encryption as an intrinsic part of the transport layer rather than an afterthought. This integration allowed for dramatic reductions in connection setup times, with QUIC supporting secure connections in a single round trip, or even enabling 0-RTT data in the case of session resumption.

This blending of transport and security reflects a broader shift in how the internet community views privacy and protection. In an age where surveillance and data breaches are rampant, QUIC makes secure-by-default a standard feature, eliminating the possibility of unencrypted fallback modes that plagued earlier protocols. The reimagined transport layer must not only be fast but inherently private and resilient against interception.

Another crucial dimension of this reimagining is QUIC's relationship with UDP. Instead of attempting to replace TCP at its own level, QUIC leverages UDP as a foundation to circumvent the ossification of TCP-centric networks. By running over UDP, QUIC sidesteps many of the middleboxes, firewalls, and NATs that are optimized for TCP behavior but indifferent to or permissive of UDP traffic. This pragmatic decision ensures that QUIC can be deployed in today's diverse internet infrastructure without waiting for a global overhaul of legacy systems.

Beyond its ability to traverse legacy networks, QUIC redefines how connections handle modern internet realities like mobility and volatility. In traditional TCP, connections are bound to IP addresses and ports, making them fragile in mobile environments where network transitions are common. When users move between networks, such as switching from Wi-Fi to cellular, TCP connections often break, forcing applications to reestablish them and endure the associated latency. QUIC, however, introduces connection identifiers that decouple the transport session from the underlying IP address, enabling seamless migration between networks. This ability to maintain stable connections across changing network conditions reflects the dynamic nature of today's mobile-first world.

Flow control and congestion control are further areas where QUIC rethinks the traditional transport model. TCP's flow control operates at the connection level, and while HTTP/2 added multiplexing at the application layer, streams still shared the same flow control mechanisms, leading to suboptimal performance under loss conditions. QUIC solves this by providing independent flow control per stream. Streams within a single QUIC connection manage their own credit independently, reducing the impact of flow control bottlenecks and enhancing overall application responsiveness. In addition, QUIC's design facilitates rapid experimentation with new congestion control algorithms, as its user-space implementation allows developers to iterate without being bound by kernel-level limitations.

This reimagined transport layer also embraces the philosophy of extensibility. QUIC is built to evolve. Its versioning system and encrypted transport parameters ensure that new extensions can be introduced without breaking compatibility with older implementations or being stifled by the middleboxes that hindered TCP's evolution. This flexibility means that QUIC can adapt over time to incorporate new cryptographic algorithms, improved congestion control mechanisms, or features tailored to emerging application demands.

Perhaps most importantly, QUIC reflects a user-centric shift in transport design. It prioritizes reducing latency, maintaining connection stability across network changes, and securing user data, all while enabling developers to fine-tune behavior for different workloads. Whether powering web browsing, file transfers, or real-time collaboration tools, the reimagined transport layer provided by QUIC aligns with the high expectations of today's internet users—expectations that demand immediacy, reliability, and trust in how data moves through the network.

The reimagined transport layer embodied by QUIC is not simply a response to the shortcomings of TCP and UDP but a proactive step forward. It recognizes that the internet's role has changed. It is no longer a static medium for information exchange but a dynamic platform supporting everything from entertainment and commerce to critical infrastructure and personal communication. As such, the transport protocols beneath this ecosystem must be equally dynamic, secure, and adaptable.

In transforming the transport layer, QUIC has also influenced how the broader internet community approaches protocol design. Its success has inspired efforts to revisit and modernize other core elements of the internet stack, setting a new standard for innovation and performance.

This reimagining of transport is not an isolated event but a catalyst for further advancements in how the internet is shaped and how it will continue to evolve in the years to come.

Connection Migration: A Game Changer

One of the most groundbreaking features of QUIC is its support for connection migration, a capability that redefines how transport protocols behave in today's mobile and multi-homed world. Connection migration refers to the ability of an active network session to seamlessly continue even when a device switches from one network interface to another, such as moving from Wi-Fi to cellular data or transitioning between different Wi-Fi networks. In traditional transport protocols like TCP, such a network change would inevitably result in a broken connection, forcing applications to re-establish the session, restart handshakes, and retransmit lost data. QUIC fundamentally changes this dynamic by allowing connections to persist across IP address changes, creating a smoother and more resilient user experience.

The need for connection migration has never been greater. The modern internet is highly mobile. Users are no longer tethered to static desktops but move between environments with varying network conditions. A person might begin streaming a video at home on Wi-Fi, walk outside while still watching the video, and switch to a mobile network without pausing. Under TCP, this transition would typically result in a dropped connection, requiring the video stream to rebuffer, renegotiate encryption keys, and restart transport sessions. The experience is disruptive and creates visible friction for end users, particularly in latency-sensitive applications such as video conferencing, online gaming, and real-time collaboration tools.

QUIC eliminates these disruptions through its use of connection identifiers, or connection IDs, which serve as stable references for ongoing sessions, independent of IP addresses or ports. Unlike TCP, which binds the session state to a specific 4-tuple—client IP, client port, server IP, server port—QUIC's design decouples transport sessions from network layer identifiers. When a client's IP address changes due to a network switch, the same connection ID can continue to be used, and the session state is preserved at both endpoints. The client simply informs the server of the new address, and the connection resumes without needing to re-establish a full handshake or renegotiate TLS parameters.

This feature is a game changer for mobile applications, which frequently face fluctuating network environments. Whether transitioning between different cellular towers or moving in and out of Wi-Fi coverage, mobile devices encounter network handoffs regularly. By supporting seamless migration, QUIC allows these handoffs to occur behind the scenes, maintaining the flow of data uninterrupted. The benefits are immediately felt by users who no longer experience the frustration of dropped calls, broken file uploads, or interrupted media streams when moving between networks.

The mechanics behind QUIC's connection migration are elegant. During the initial handshake, clients and servers exchange connection IDs that are used throughout the life of the session. When the client detects a change in its local network conditions—such as receiving a new IP address from a mobile carrier—it can initiate a path update by sending a QUIC packet from the new address while maintaining the same connection ID. The server, upon receiving this packet, can verify that the client is still in control of the session and continue communication over the new path. This verification step is critical to preventing malicious actors from hijacking sessions by spoofing addresses.

Security is a central consideration in QUIC's migration process. To guard against connection hijacking and amplification attacks, QUIC mandates address validation before allowing data transmission over a new path. Typically, this involves the server issuing a token to the client during the initial handshake, which the client must present when attempting to migrate the connection. This token serves as proof that the client was reachable at its prior address and helps prevent attackers from injecting forged migration attempts.

Beyond improving user experience, connection migration enhances resource efficiency at both client and server levels. In traditional TCP-based systems, frequent network changes would result in many half-open or abruptly terminated connections, consuming server resources and complicating session management. QUIC's migration capability reduces the number of abandoned connections and minimizes the overhead associated with re-establishing sessions, improving both performance and scalability for large-scale services.

Connection migration also opens new doors for multi-homed devices—those with multiple active network interfaces, such as laptops or smartphones that have both Wi-Fi and cellular capabilities. In future implementations, QUIC could support simultaneous multi-path connections, where data flows are distributed across multiple networks concurrently. Although QUIC's standard migration feature focuses on switching paths rather than multipath aggregation, its flexibility and extensibility create opportunities for future enhancements that could resemble or even surpass the capabilities seen in Multipath TCP.

In addition to its immediate practical benefits, connection migration represents a philosophical shift in transport protocol design. For decades, the transport layer assumed a largely static model, where connections were tied to stable IP addresses for the duration of a session. This model no longer reflects the realities of modern networking. Today's users are on the move, applications are dynamic, and network environments are unpredictable. By embracing mobility as a core design consideration, QUIC realigns the transport layer with contemporary needs, delivering a protocol that is as mobile as its users.

From a developer's perspective, connection migration simplifies application design. Developers no longer need to build custom logic to detect and recover from broken connections caused by network changes. Applications can rely on QUIC's built-in mechanisms to handle path migration, reducing complexity and shortening development cycles. This ease of use, coupled with improved user experience, makes QUIC an attractive choice for real-time applications, cloud services, and emerging technologies like augmented and virtual reality, which demand seamless, high-performance connectivity.

The impact of connection migration is already being felt across services that have adopted QUIC. Video streaming platforms, messaging apps, and large-scale cloud applications benefit from fewer session drops, lower reconnection latency, and more consistent user engagement. In live streaming and video conferencing, for example, connection migration can mean the difference between a smooth, uninterrupted meeting and one marred by awkward pauses and reconnection attempts when participants change networks.

Connection migration ultimately represents more than just a technical feature—it is a fundamental enhancement to how the internet works in an increasingly mobile world. It reflects an understanding that network transitions should be invisible to users and that applications should continue to perform reliably no matter how often the underlying path changes. By addressing a challenge that has long hindered TCP-based communications, QUIC not only improves performance but also helps fulfill the modern internet's promise of always-on, always-connected services. In doing so, connection migration positions QUIC as a transport protocol built for the realities and expectations of today's global internet users.

Built for Mobile and Modern Networks

The architecture of QUIC is a direct response to the realities of mobile and modern networks. The landscape of internet usage has undergone a radical transformation in recent years. Gone are the days when users primarily accessed the web from stationary desktop computers tethered to wired connections. Today, the majority of internet traffic originates from mobile devices, which connect through wireless networks that are inherently unstable, lossy, and variable in performance. This shift has fundamentally changed the requirements for transport protocols. A modern transport layer must handle unpredictable latency, fluctuating bandwidth, and frequent changes in network paths, all while delivering secure, low-latency, and seamless experiences. QUIC was designed from the ground up to meet these challenges, making it a protocol that feels native to the demands of mobile-first and modern network environments.

Wireless networks, such as LTE, 5G, and Wi-Fi, present a unique set of obstacles for traditional protocols like TCP. Variable signal strength, handoffs between cell towers, interference, and packet loss are common. TCP, which was built in an era of more stable, wired networks, often struggles under these conditions. Its conservative congestion control algorithms, head-of-line blocking issues, and reliance on fixed IP addresses make it ill-suited to the dynamic nature of mobile connectivity. QUIC addresses these shortcomings with a suite of innovations specifically tailored for such environments.

One of QUIC's core advantages is its resilience to packet loss, which is a frequent occurrence in mobile networks. TCP's design forces all streams within a connection to wait for the retransmission of a lost packet, introducing delays and jitter, which degrade user experience, especially in real-time applications like video calls or online gaming. QUIC's multiplexed stream model eliminates transport-level head-of-line blocking by allowing each stream within a connection to operate independently. When a packet carrying data for one stream is lost, other streams can continue transmitting without waiting. This behavior results in a smoother, more responsive experience even when network conditions are suboptimal.

QUIC also excels in reducing latency, a critical factor in mobile environments where every round trip between client and server counts. Traditional TCP connections require a three-way handshake, followed by a separate TLS handshake, before data can be securely exchanged. This multi-step process compounds latency, especially in high round-trip-time scenarios common in mobile networks. QUIC streamlines this process by combining transport and encryption handshakes into a single event. In many cases, QUIC can establish secure connections with a single round trip or even zero round trips for resumed sessions. This reduced handshake latency translates directly into faster load times for web pages, quicker video starts, and snappier application responses on mobile devices.

In addition to tackling latency and packet loss, QUIC addresses another critical challenge in mobile networks: network transitions. Mobile devices frequently move between networks, such as switching from Wi-Fi to cellular data or between different cellular networks as a user travels. TCP ties the connection state to a specific IP address and port, so a change in the device's network requires tearing down the connection and establishing a new one. This process leads to noticeable interruptions, forcing users to endure delays, reconnect attempts, and in some cases, data loss.

QUIC, by contrast, introduces connection migration as a built-in feature. Using connection IDs that remain stable even as the device's IP address changes, QUIC enables active sessions to persist across network transitions. Whether a user is walking out of a building while streaming a video or moving from a home Wi-Fi network to a mobile network during a video call, QUIC maintains the session without breaking. This seamless migration capability is a direct response to the realities of mobile internet usage, where continuity and stability are critical to a positive user experience.

Modern networks also exhibit significant variability in bandwidth. Mobile networks may fluctuate depending on network congestion, signal interference, and user mobility. QUIC's design enables adaptive congestion control mechanisms that can be tuned to these conditions. Unlike TCP, which is often bound by ossified kernel-level implementations, QUIC's user-space design allows developers to deploy and iterate on advanced congestion control algorithms like BBR more quickly. These algorithms are designed to make better use of available bandwidth, avoid unnecessary retransmissions, and adapt dynamically to network fluctuations, helping maintain high throughput and low latency even in unstable network conditions.

Security is another cornerstone of QUIC's suitability for modern networks. Mobile networks are inherently less secure than wired ones, and users often connect through public Wi-Fi hotspots or shared cellular infrastructure, where the risk of eavesdropping or man-in-the-middle attacks is elevated. By making encryption mandatory and embedding TLS 1.3 directly into its transport layer, QUIC ensures that every connection is protected by default. This protects users from common attack vectors present in wireless environments and reinforces modern security expectations, where end-to-end encryption is no longer optional but essential.

Beyond individual users, QUIC is also designed with the cloud-driven nature of modern applications in mind. Services today are distributed, often relying on edge computing, content delivery networks (CDNs), and multi-region cloud deployments to bring data closer to users and reduce latency. QUIC's ability to rapidly establish connections, recover gracefully from packet loss, and migrate connections across network paths aligns perfectly with these architectural trends. In large-scale distributed systems, where performance optimizations at the transport layer can yield significant benefits, QUIC provides the agility and efficiency needed to operate across heterogeneous and often unpredictable network environments.

Developers building for modern networks also benefit from QUIC's extensibility. Its modular design allows for experimentation and customization to suit specific application needs, whether that means fine-tuning congestion control for streaming applications, optimizing stream prioritization for web content delivery, or incorporating custom transport-level signals for emerging technologies like augmented reality, virtual reality, or IoT ecosystems.

The mobile-first world has exposed the weaknesses of legacy transport protocols and created an urgent need for a transport layer that can handle instability, mobility, and unpredictability with ease. QUIC was built with these realities at its core. Its capabilities are not just theoretical but have proven effective in production environments across services such as Google Search, YouTube, and various CDN platforms, where QUIC has consistently delivered faster load times, smoother media playback, and more reliable application performance, especially for users on mobile networks.

QUIC's ability to adapt to the challenges of mobile and modern networks positions it as the transport protocol of choice for the next generation of internet applications. It bridges the gap between the old assumptions of static, wired networks and the dynamic, mobile-centric world we now inhabit. Whether supporting users streaming high-definition videos while commuting or enabling enterprises to deliver secure, low-latency services to customers across the globe, QUIC represents a redefinition of how transport protocols can—and should—work in today's connected society.

Flow Control and Congestion Control in QUIC

One of the defining features of QUIC is its sophisticated approach to flow control and congestion control, two mechanisms that are essential to the efficient and reliable delivery of data across the internet. While these mechanisms have been fundamental to transport protocols for decades, QUIC introduces important innovations that provide improved performance, flexibility, and adaptability to modern network environments. Flow control and congestion control serve different purposes, yet they are tightly interwoven. Flow control manages how much data a sender is allowed to transmit to ensure that the receiver can handle incoming data without overwhelming its buffers. Congestion control, on the other hand, governs how much data a sender can inject into the network to avoid contributing to congestion in the underlying infrastructure. Together, these mechanisms protect both endpoints and the network itself from overload and inefficiencies.

In traditional TCP, flow control operates at the connection level. A receiver advertises a single window size, indicating how much data the sender can transmit before awaiting acknowledgment that some of the data has been processed. This design works reasonably well for simple applications but becomes suboptimal when multiplexing multiple streams over a single TCP connection, as seen in HTTP/2. Because TCP does not differentiate between streams at the transport layer, all streams share the same flow control window. This means that a slow-consuming or stalled stream can inadvertently restrict the progress of unrelated streams sharing the same connection, leading to inefficient bandwidth usage.

QUIC addresses this limitation by introducing stream-level flow control. Each stream within a QUIC connection maintains its own independent flow control window, separate from the connection-level limits. This per-stream granularity allows QUIC to optimize data delivery for multiplexed applications, such as modern web browsers fetching dozens of resources simultaneously. If one stream encounters backpressure because the application is slow to process its data, other streams can continue transmitting data freely, without being blocked by the stalled stream. This feature dramatically enhances responsiveness and efficiency, particularly in complex applications like single-page web apps or real-time collaboration platforms where many independent data streams may be active at once.

Complementing its improved flow control design, QUIC also implements robust congestion control mechanisms. QUIC, unlike TCP, is implemented in user space, enabling developers to quickly iterate on and deploy advanced congestion control algorithms. This flexibility allows QUIC to move beyond the limitations imposed by TCP's slow adoption cycles and ossified infrastructure. While QUIC can utilize traditional algorithms such as Reno or Cubic, it is often paired with newer approaches like Google's BBR (Bottleneck Bandwidth and Round-trip propagation time). BBR takes a proactive stance, estimating available bandwidth and network latency to achieve higher throughput with lower queuing delay. BBR's ability to keep queues short while maximizing link utilization makes it well-suited for modern applications, particularly in networks where latency and bandwidth vary, such as mobile and wireless environments.

Another innovation in QUIC's congestion control lies in its integration with the packet-level structure of the protocol. QUIC employs packet numbers to track individual packets across all streams, making congestion control more granular and responsive. Unlike TCP, where loss is inferred from missing acknowledgments on a single byte stream, QUIC can assess packet loss on a per-packet basis. This allows QUIC's congestion control to make more informed decisions when adjusting transmission rates, leading to faster recovery from loss and better adaptation to network conditions. Additionally, QUIC's acknowledgment frames can include more detailed information about received packets, such as the receipt times of multiple packets in a single acknowledgment. This richer feedback allows for more accurate round-trip time measurements and fine-tuning of congestion windows.

The independence between flow control and congestion control in QUIC also grants developers greater control over the behavior of applications. Flow control is predominantly concerned with application-level constraints, ensuring that receivers are not overwhelmed by incoming data. Congestion control, meanwhile, is focused on being a responsible network citizen, adjusting send rates based on the health of the underlying network. By separating these concerns, QUIC allows for more nuanced behavior. For example, a receiver with limited memory can advertise a small flow control window for certain streams, while the sender can still take advantage of available network bandwidth for other streams that the receiver is ready to process.

One of the most impactful benefits of QUIC's design is its ability to minimize head-of-line blocking, not only at the stream level but also in terms of congestion recovery. TCP's head-of-line blocking, where packet loss stalls the entire byte stream, introduces significant latency spikes, especially over lossy networks. In QUIC, the stream-level independence combined with packet-level recovery ensures that loss affecting one stream or a subset of packets does not stall unrelated streams. This design choice is particularly valuable in applications that require real-time responsiveness, such as voice-over-IP, online gaming, and interactive media services.

Furthermore, QUIC's user-space implementation empowers application developers to deploy custom congestion control algorithms tailored to specific workloads. In environments like cloud data centers, developers may prefer algorithms optimized for high-throughput and low-latency scenarios, while applications targeting mobile users in emerging markets might select algorithms that prioritize robustness under high packet loss and variable bandwidth conditions. This adaptability positions QUIC as a versatile solution capable of meeting diverse application requirements without waiting for wide-scale OS updates.

QUIC also incorporates mechanisms to handle connection-level flow control, which governs the aggregate data limits across all streams in a connection. This ensures that even if individual streams are well-behaved, the connection as a whole does not overwhelm the receiver. Connection-level flow control provides a backstop against excessive memory usage and ensures that total outstanding data remains within manageable bounds.

As networks continue to evolve, particularly with the rollout of 5G and the increasing reliance on Wi-Fi 6 and other advanced wireless technologies, the variability in available bandwidth and latency will persist. QUIC's modern approach to flow control and congestion control ensures that applications built on top of it can continue to perform optimally in these environments. Whether traversing congested urban cellular networks or delivering data across high-speed fiber links, QUIC's mechanisms allow for agile adaptation to network conditions while maintaining fairness and stability across the network.

Flow control and congestion control in QUIC exemplify how rethinking long-standing internet mechanisms can yield significant improvements in performance and reliability. By focusing on stream independence, granular packet feedback, and extensibility, QUIC delivers a transport protocol that is ready to meet the challenges of today's highly dynamic and demanding internet landscape. It represents a forward-looking vision where transport protocols are no longer a bottleneck but an enabler of seamless, efficient, and responsive digital experiences.

Stream Prioritization and Fairness

In the design of QUIC, stream prioritization and fairness are two crucial concepts that directly impact the performance, efficiency, and user experience of modern applications. As web applications and online services have grown more complex, they increasingly rely on the simultaneous transmission of multiple independent streams of data. Whether fetching numerous assets on a webpage, managing real-time communication streams, or handling large file transfers alongside background data synchronization, managing how these streams interact within a single connection has become essential. QUIC, with its multiplexed stream model, offers a unique opportunity to address this challenge by enabling smarter stream prioritization and ensuring fairness across streams, ultimately making the network more responsive to user needs.

Stream prioritization refers to the ability to control the order and importance of data delivery across multiple streams within a single QUIC connection. Not all data streams in a modern application are equally important. For example, when loading a web page, the HTML document and critical CSS resources are far more important than background images or analytics scripts. In video conferencing, voice data may need to take precedence over screen-sharing streams to ensure clear communication. By giving applications fine-grained control over which streams should be prioritized, QUIC helps developers improve the responsiveness and usability of their services.

Unlike TCP, which only provides a single ordered byte stream and leaves multiplexing to higher layers like HTTP/2, QUIC natively supports multiple independent streams within a connection. This architectural choice allows stream prioritization to be handled at the transport layer itself. Each stream within QUIC can progress independently, and each stream's flow control is distinct from others. This independence removes the limitations imposed by TCP's head-of-line blocking, where one delayed packet could hold up unrelated data streams. In QUIC, a high-priority stream can continue without being impeded by packet loss or congestion affecting a lower-priority stream.

QUIC itself does not enforce a strict prioritization mechanism within its core specification. Instead, it provides the building blocks for applications to implement their own prioritization logic. This design allows flexibility for different use cases. HTTP/3, which runs atop QUIC, is one prominent example where prioritization schemes have been developed to optimize resource delivery in web applications. In HTTP/3, streams corresponding to critical resources, such as HTML or JavaScript necessary for rendering a page, can be prioritized over auxiliary resources like third-party trackers or decorative images. This ensures that essential content is delivered and processed first, reducing page load times and enhancing perceived performance.

Fairness, on the other hand, is the principle that all streams within a connection—or between different connections—should have equitable access to shared resources such as available bandwidth or connection window space. In practical terms, fairness ensures that no single stream monopolizes all network capacity at the expense of others. This is particularly important in complex web applications, where both foreground and background activities compete for attention. QUIC's per-stream flow control helps enforce fairness at the transport layer by ensuring that flow control limits are honored individually per stream, preventing aggressive streams from starving others.

Maintaining fairness across streams also plays a critical role in real-time applications. In video conferencing or multiplayer gaming, fairness guarantees that control messages and small, time-sensitive data packets are not delayed by bulk data transfers. For instance, in a video call where video frames and audio packets share a connection with file-sharing streams, fairness mechanisms ensure that audio packets, which are highly sensitive to latency, receive timely delivery even if a large file is being transferred in parallel.

QUIC's congestion control algorithms further contribute to fairness. Since QUIC operates in user space and is extensible, it allows applications to experiment with congestion control strategies that balance performance and fairness more effectively than traditional TCP implementations. Congestion control in QUIC operates at the connection level, but applications can leverage this control to adjust stream behaviors dynamically. For example, developers can implement priority-based scheduling that favors interactive streams over bulk transfers while still respecting the global congestion control parameters that prevent network overload.

Stream prioritization and fairness in QUIC also extend to scenarios involving network variability and mobile environments. Mobile users frequently experience changing bandwidth conditions due to fluctuating signal strength or transitions between networks. In these cases, effective prioritization ensures that essential streams, such as audio in a video call, remain unaffected even if the network suddenly becomes congested or unstable. By intelligently allocating resources to high-priority streams first, QUIC enhances the resilience of applications under adverse network conditions, maintaining service quality without dropping critical data.

The benefits of QUIC's prioritization model are magnified when combined with modern web technologies. Single-page applications, progressive web apps, and dynamic content delivery models rely heavily on loading many resources concurrently. In these environments, efficient prioritization can dramatically affect user experience. By ensuring that core scripts and content load before background tasks, developers can optimize perceived page speed and responsiveness, reducing bounce rates and improving engagement.

Fairness is equally important when considering multi-tenant environments such as cloud platforms, content delivery networks, and edge computing services. In these settings, servers often handle numerous QUIC connections from different clients simultaneously. Implementing fairness at the connection level—ensuring that one client does not consume an outsized share of resources to the detriment of others—is critical for maintaining performance across a large user base. QUIC's extensibility allows server operators to develop scheduling and resource allocation strategies that promote fairness between connections while still respecting each client's prioritization needs within their individual streams.

Another dimension where QUIC's prioritization capabilities stand out is in media delivery. Video streaming services can leverage QUIC's stream management to prioritize keyframes or audio tracks over less critical video frames, minimizing the perceptual impact of network fluctuations. This improves the overall quality of experience for users consuming video content on networks with variable capacity, such as mobile or satellite connections.

As developers adopt QUIC and explore its full potential, the interplay between prioritization and fairness will become even more important. Emerging applications such as augmented reality, virtual reality, and interactive cloud-based environments demand precise control over which data arrives first and how bandwidth is shared across competing tasks. QUIC's design provides the foundation for these use cases, enabling developers to build applications that feel faster, more reliable, and more responsive even under network stress.

Ultimately, stream prioritization and fairness are not merely technical considerations within QUIC; they are key enablers of the user-centric performance improvements that modern internet applications require. By giving developers the tools to balance competing demands across multiple streams, QUIC helps create digital experiences that are smooth, efficient, and respectful of the network's limitations. In doing so, it elevates the transport layer into an active participant in shaping the responsiveness and quality of the modern web.

The Role of Frames in QUIC

In the architecture of QUIC, frames play a central role in how data and control information are structured, transmitted, and processed. Frames are the fundamental units of communication within QUIC packets, serving as the protocol's internal building blocks. Unlike traditional transport protocols like TCP, which operate over a continuous byte stream and lack an inherent framing structure, QUIC takes a modular approach by defining specific frame types for distinct functions. This decision enables a level of flexibility, efficiency, and extensibility that sets QUIC apart from its predecessors.

Each QUIC packet can contain one or more frames, each responsible for carrying either application-level data or transport-level control information. By allowing multiple frames to coexist within a single packet, QUIC maximizes the use of available packet space and minimizes the number of packets needed to achieve specific communication goals. This helps reduce overhead, optimize bandwidth usage, and improve the responsiveness of the protocol, especially in latency-sensitive applications.

The most common frame type in QUIC is the STREAM frame. STREAM frames are responsible for transmitting application data, such as HTTP/3 payloads, over a given stream within a QUIC connection. Each STREAM frame includes identifiers that indicate which stream the frame belongs to, an offset that specifies where the data fits within the stream's sequence, and flags that signal whether the frame marks the end of the stream. This framing approach allows for fine-grained control over how application data is delivered. Since streams are independent in QUIC, the transport of one stream's frames does not block or interfere with others, preventing head-of-line blocking at the transport layer. The use of STREAM frames enables multiplexing of multiple streams over a single connection while preserving their independence and ensuring that lost packets affect only the streams to which they belong.

Beyond STREAM frames, QUIC employs a variety of control frames that manage the behavior and state of the connection itself. For example, the ACK frame is a critical component of QUIC's reliability and congestion control mechanisms. ACK frames inform the sender which packets have been successfully received, including additional metadata such as acknowledgment delay and selective acknowledgment ranges. By leveraging ACK frames, QUIC can efficiently track packet loss, adjust congestion windows, and trigger retransmissions when necessary. The rich information provided by ACK frames enables QUIC's congestion control algorithms to make more informed decisions, resulting in faster recovery from loss events and more adaptive behavior in fluctuating network environments.

Another essential control frame is the MAX_STREAM_DATA frame, which contributes to QUIC's flow control mechanisms. This frame communicates the flow control window for a specific stream, informing the sender how much additional data it is permitted to transmit on that stream. Similarly, the MAX_DATA frame sets flow control limits for the entire connection, ensuring that the receiver is not overwhelmed by excessive incoming data. These frames allow receivers to dynamically adjust flow control limits based on their current capacity and application requirements. By decoupling flow control at both the stream and connection levels, QUIC empowers applications to balance resource usage and optimize performance.

The PING frame serves a different but equally important role, helping maintain connection liveness. In periods of inactivity, endpoints can send PING frames to elicit a response from their peer, confirming that the connection is still functional. This is especially valuable in scenarios where long-lived connections are used, such as in persistent HTTP/3 sessions or real-time communications. PING frames help detect connection failures in a timely manner and facilitate rapid recovery strategies.

The CONNECTION_CLOSE frame is used to gracefully terminate a QUIC connection. When a peer determines that a connection should be closed, it sends a CONNECTION_CLOSE frame to notify the other endpoint of the shutdown, including an error code and an optional reason phrase. This explicit signaling of connection termination is an improvement over TCP's abrupt connection resets and provides additional context that can be useful for debugging, monitoring, and managing connection lifecycle events.

Another noteworthy frame is the PATH_CHALLENGE frame, which plays a critical role in QUIC's connection migration and path validation features. When a client moves to a new network path, such as switching from Wi-Fi to cellular data, it can send a PATH_CHALLENGE frame to verify that the new path is functional and that the peer can receive packets at the new address. The peer responds with a PATH_RESPONSE frame, completing the validation process and allowing data transfer to resume on the new path. These frames are instrumental in enabling QUIC's seamless connection migration, which is essential for supporting mobile users who frequently move between different networks.

The CRYPTO frame is another key element, carrying handshake data required for establishing the TLS 1.3-encrypted session that secures the QUIC connection. Unlike TCP, where the TLS handshake occurs separately after the connection is established, QUIC integrates the TLS handshake directly into its transport layer using CRYPTO frames. This integration reduces handshake latency and simplifies session establishment by combining transport and security negotiations into a unified process.

Additionally, the NEW_CONNECTION_ID frame is used to manage connection identifiers. During the lifetime of a QUIC connection, an endpoint can issue new connection IDs using this frame, allowing for more robust connection migration strategies and enhanced resistance to certain types of attacks, such as linkability between different network paths.

The modular design of frames in QUIC extends to extensibility as well. The protocol was built with the expectation that new frame types could be added in the future without breaking existing implementations. Frames are self-describing, meaning each frame type includes its own type field, allowing receivers to safely ignore unknown or unsupported frames while processing those they understand. This characteristic ensures that QUIC can evolve over time to meet emerging application needs, incorporate new features, or respond to changing security and performance requirements without requiring disruptive changes to the protocol's core.

The role of frames in QUIC exemplifies the protocol's modern design philosophy: modular, efficient, and adaptable. Frames allow QUIC to serve as a transport protocol that is not only fast and reliable but also highly customizable to meet the diverse demands of today's applications. From facilitating multiplexed data delivery to enabling advanced features like connection migration and encrypted handshakes, frames are the mechanism through which QUIC's many innovations are realized.

As the internet continues to evolve, frames provide QUIC with a flexible framework to adapt to the needs of future applications and network environments. Whether supporting web browsers fetching complex pages, media streaming platforms delivering seamless content, or real-time applications ensuring uninterrupted communications, frames are the fundamental unit that makes QUIC's high performance and modern capabilities possible.

Packet Number Spaces Explained

One of the most innovative aspects of QUIC's design is its use of distinct packet number spaces. This concept, though technical in nature, plays a critical role in how QUIC achieves faster connection setup, more efficient loss recovery, and robust security compared to traditional transport protocols. Packet numbers in any protocol help endpoints track the delivery of packets, detect loss, and maintain the proper order of communication. However, QUIC takes this to another level by defining multiple, separate packet number spaces, each dedicated to different stages or aspects of the connection lifecycle.

In QUIC, packet numbers are not continuous across the entire lifetime of a connection. Instead, they are divided into three distinct packet number spaces: Initial, Handshake, and 1-RTT (one round-trip time). Each space has its own independent sequence of packet numbers, starting at zero, and each serves a specific purpose in the protocol's progression from connection establishment to encrypted application data transmission.

The Initial packet number space is used at the very beginning of the connection. When a client initiates a QUIC connection, it sends an Initial packet containing the first messages of the TLS 1.3 handshake, encapsulated within QUIC's CRYPTO frame. This packet is essential for bootstrapping the encrypted session. Because Initial packets must be readable by the server before a shared encryption context is fully established, they are encrypted using a set of provisional keys derived from publicly known information, such as the connection ID. All packets exchanged during this Initial phase belong to the Initial packet number space, and the numbers increment independently from those used later in the connection.

Following the Initial space, the Handshake packet number space comes into play. Handshake packets continue the TLS handshake process, including the exchange of server certificates and the negotiation of session keys. These packets are encrypted with stronger keys derived from the completed TLS key exchange. The Handshake space is isolated from both the Initial and 1-RTT spaces, ensuring that packets carrying handshake data do not interfere with packet loss detection or acknowledgment logic associated with other stages of the connection. The separation of the Handshake packet number space is a deliberate design choice to enhance security and reliability, preventing any confusion about which packets correspond to which phase of the handshake.

Once the TLS handshake is complete, the connection transitions to the 1-RTT packet number space. This space is dedicated to carrying fully encrypted application data, such as HTTP/3 requests and responses, as well as transport-level frames that manage stream state, flow control, and connection health. The 1-RTT space is where the bulk of a QUIC connection's activity occurs. From this point forward, all packets are protected using the strongest set of encryption keys, and the packet numbers increment independently from the Initial and Handshake spaces.

The separation of packet number spaces is a sharp contrast to TCP, which maintains a single, continuous sequence number space across the lifetime of a connection. In TCP, sequence numbers apply equally to handshake messages, control messages, and application data, creating a monolithic flow of bytes that can complicate loss recovery and retransmission logic. By segmenting these phases in QUIC, each stage of the connection benefits from more targeted mechanisms for loss detection, congestion control, and security.

One key advantage of using separate packet number spaces is in the handling of retransmissions and acknowledgments. For example, if a packet is lost during the Initial stage, only packets within the Initial space will be retransmitted, and acknowledgments will be scoped to that space. This ensures that handshake retransmissions do not interfere with or delay the transition to application data exchange in the 1-RTT space. Similarly, any packet loss detected in the 1-RTT space is handled independently, reducing the likelihood of cascading delays or head-of-line blocking across the entire connection.

This design also improves QUIC's ability to defend against certain types of attacks. For instance, a common threat in legacy protocols is the potential for attackers to inject or replay handshake packets after the handshake has completed. In QUIC, the separation of packet number spaces means that once the connection has transitioned to the 1-RTT space, any packets from the Initial or Handshake spaces are automatically ignored, as they no longer apply to the active session. This prevents older handshake data from disrupting or corrupting the encrypted data stream, reinforcing QUIC's security model.

The packet number spaces also serve an important role in optimizing connection setup times. Because the TLS handshake is carried out concurrently with the QUIC transport handshake, separating packet spaces allows both processes to proceed without interference. For example, acknowledgments for Initial packets can be processed independently of Handshake packets, allowing the TLS key exchange to complete more quickly and facilitating faster transition to fully encrypted data exchange. This enables QUIC to establish secure connections in fewer round trips compared to the traditional TCP and TLS stack, contributing to QUIC's reputation for low-latency performance.

The use of multiple packet number spaces also benefits the encryption layer itself. QUIC encrypts each packet's payload and most of its header fields, including the packet number, using keys specific to the corresponding space. This means that packets in the Initial space are encrypted differently from those in the Handshake or 1-RTT spaces. As a result, even if an attacker were able to observe and correlate packet numbers from different stages of the connection, they would gain little actionable information. Encryption of the packet number also helps obscure connection behavior from passive observers, enhancing user privacy.

From an implementation perspective, packet number spaces add complexity to the design of a QUIC stack. Developers must ensure that their loss detection and retransmission logic properly track each space separately, maintaining distinct acknowledgment records and recovery timers. However, this complexity is offset by the operational advantages and performance improvements delivered by the model. The clean division between stages simplifies reasoning about connection behavior, makes state management more robust, and enables a more modular and extensible protocol design.

Ultimately, the introduction of distinct packet number spaces within QUIC reflects a modern, security-conscious approach to transport protocol design. It offers a more granular and resilient foundation for handling the variety of challenges present in today's internet—whether that be loss-prone mobile networks, adversarial environments, or the need for lightning-fast connection setup times. This architectural choice underscores QUIC's commitment to rethinking transport protocols in ways that enhance performance, security, and adaptability for the next generation of internet applications.

Stateless Reset and Connection Resilience

A defining attribute of QUIC's architecture is its ability to provide connection resilience in the face of network disruptions, server failures, and abrupt session terminations. One key mechanism that contributes to this resilience is the stateless reset. In contrast to traditional protocols like TCP, where connection teardown and error handling rely heavily on connection state stored at both endpoints, QUIC introduces a novel stateless reset mechanism that enhances the protocol's robustness while reducing the resource burden on servers. At its core, the stateless reset allows a server to terminate a connection without retaining session state, all while providing the client with enough information to detect and respond appropriately to the reset.

The stateless reset is essential in situations where a server loses its internal state due to a crash, reboot, or intentional configuration change. In TCP, a client might continue to send packets to a server that no longer remembers the session, resulting in half-open connections or blackhole scenarios where the client's packets go unanswered. The client would have to rely on timeouts or heuristics to eventually detect the connection failure, leading to poor responsiveness and degraded user experience. QUIC addresses this by enabling servers to issue a stateless reset response that informs the client unequivocally that the connection no longer exists.

Unlike a typical connection termination that would require maintaining connection-specific data, a stateless reset allows the server to terminate connections purely based on stateless information derived from the incoming packet itself. QUIC achieves this by associating each connection ID with a stateless reset token generated by the server. This token is a random-looking value derived from a secure, server-wide secret and is included in the connection state sent to the client. The server does not need to retain this token; it can regenerate it on demand based on the connection ID, enabling the server to issue stateless resets even after discarding the session's runtime state.

When a server receives a packet with an unknown or expired connection ID, it can reply with a stateless reset packet. This packet is indistinguishable from a short header QUIC packet at first glance, containing a random-looking payload followed by the reset token. Upon receipt, the client validates the reset token against the one it has previously associated with the server's connection ID. If the tokens match, the client knows that the server has forcibly closed the connection and immediately terminates the session, releasing associated resources and preventing further retransmissions.

The stateless reset plays a vital role in maintaining efficiency and scalability, particularly for high-traffic servers such as those operated by content delivery networks, large-scale web services, or cloud providers. These servers may handle millions of concurrent QUIC connections. Without stateless resets, servers would be forced to retain connection state longer than necessary or risk leaving clients in a limbo state. By enabling stateless resets, servers can safely discard connection state when needed, secure in the knowledge that clients will be able to detect and respond to resets without ambiguity.

The resilience offered by stateless resets extends beyond server restarts. They are especially useful in load-balanced environments where connection IDs might be distributed across multiple backend servers. If a load balancer incorrectly routes packets from an active client to a backend server that does not recognize the connection, that backend can issue a stateless reset, prompting the client to re-establish the connection. This avoids silent packet drops and reduces failover times, helping maintain the responsiveness and reliability of distributed services.

Another advantage of the stateless reset mechanism is its synergy with QUIC's connection migration feature. While connection migration allows clients to continue a session across network changes—such as switching from Wi-Fi to mobile data—there are cases where migration fails or is misrouted. In such situations, a server receiving packets on an unfamiliar path can issue a stateless reset, ensuring that clients detect the failure promptly and can attempt to reconnect through a valid path or fallback protocol like TCP.

Security considerations are a critical part of QUIC's stateless reset design. Stateless resets are intentionally indistinguishable from short header packets to passive observers, preventing attackers from identifying them easily in network traffic and using them as signals to infer information about connection lifetimes or server behaviors. Additionally, reset tokens are designed to be unforgeable, relying on cryptographic methods that make it infeasible for attackers to generate valid reset tokens without access to the server's secret.

However, the very power of stateless resets comes with risks if improperly used. Malicious actors who gain control of a server's keying material could abuse stateless resets to prematurely close client connections. For this reason, server operators must protect reset token generation secrets with the same rigor as TLS keys. Furthermore, clients must implement stateless reset handling carefully to avoid scenarios where false positives could disrupt active sessions.

Beyond failure recovery, stateless resets contribute to the protocol's robustness under adversarial network conditions. In hostile environments where packets are deliberately dropped or manipulated, QUIC's stateless reset mechanism enables faster detection of connection invalidation compared to relying solely on retransmission timers or transport-layer keepalives. This capability is particularly valuable in mobile and satellite networks, where disruptions and path changes occur frequently, and waiting for a timeout could introduce noticeable delays.

Stateless resets also integrate well with QUIC's philosophy of end-to-end control and minimal reliance on network intermediaries. In traditional TCP, middleboxes often attempt to manage connection state, sometimes injecting TCP RST packets to forcefully close connections based on predefined heuristics. QUIC, with its encrypted transport headers and stateless reset mechanism, ensures that connection management remains largely between the client and the server, reducing the influence of middleboxes and enhancing privacy and control.

Ultimately, stateless resets are a cornerstone of QUIC's strategy to deliver high-performance, resilient connections in today's complex and ever-changing network environments. They provide a clear, secure, and efficient mechanism for handling unexpected disconnections, freeing servers from the burden of long-lived state retention, and giving clients fast feedback when something goes wrong. This capability aligns perfectly with QUIC's broader goals: a transport protocol that is not only fast and secure but also designed to thrive in the diverse, mobile, and distributed nature of the modern internet.

Loss Detection and Recovery in QUIC

Loss detection and recovery are fundamental components of any reliable transport protocol, and QUIC introduces significant advancements in how these processes are handled. While TCP relies on mechanisms like duplicate acknowledgments and timeouts to detect packet loss, QUIC leverages its modern design to implement a more nuanced and efficient approach. QUIC's packet-based model, its rich acknowledgment signals, and its flexible user-space architecture allow for faster, more accurate detection of packet loss and more efficient recovery, especially over networks where latency, jitter, and packet loss are common.

At the core of QUIC's loss detection system is its use of packet numbers. Every QUIC packet, regardless of the stream it belongs to, is assigned a unique, strictly increasing packet number. This packet-level granularity stands in contrast to TCP's byte-oriented sequence numbers and helps QUIC detect missing packets with greater precision. Because QUIC multiplexes multiple independent streams over a single connection, this packet-level loss detection mechanism ensures that issues on one stream do not introduce unnecessary delays for other streams, helping eliminate the head-of-line blocking problem that plagues TCP.

When a packet is sent in QUIC, it is considered "in-flight" until the sender receives an acknowledgment from the receiver. QUIC's acknowledgment frames (ACK frames) provide detailed feedback on which specific packets have been received successfully, as well as which packets appear to be missing. Unlike TCP's cumulative acknowledgment model, where a single acknowledgment covers all bytes up to a certain sequence number, QUIC's selective acknowledgment model allows endpoints to communicate gaps in packet reception explicitly. ACK frames in QUIC also include acknowledgment delay information and can contain multiple acknowledgment ranges, providing the sender with a granular view of which packets arrived and which did not.

This rich acknowledgment signaling allows QUIC's loss detection algorithm to operate more responsively and avoid false positives. For instance, if packets 1, 2, and 4 are acknowledged, but packet 3 is missing from the acknowledgment range, the sender immediately infers that packet 3 has likely been lost. In TCP, the sender might wait for multiple duplicate acknowledgments or a timeout to detect such loss, delaying retransmission. QUIC's precise feedback loop enables faster detection and recovery, reducing the impact of loss on application-level performance.

Another key feature of QUIC's loss detection system is its reliance on a hybrid model that incorporates both time-based and acknowledgment-based heuristics. QUIC uses timers to detect loss, but these timers are informed by real-time measurements of the connection's round-trip time (RTT) and its variance. By maintaining an accurate and adaptive RTT estimate, QUIC can set more intelligent and context-aware timers that balance responsiveness with network conditions. This model allows QUIC to detect loss swiftly on low-latency links while avoiding premature retransmissions on high-latency or high-jitter networks.

In addition to packet loss detection, QUIC is designed to recover from loss efficiently. Once a packet is deemed lost, the sender schedules a retransmission of the necessary frames. Importantly, QUIC retransmits the frames—not the original packet itself—allowing greater flexibility. Since QUIC operates with a frame-based architecture, lost frames can be repackaged into new packets alongside other frames, optimizing packet utilization and reducing overhead. This behavior contrasts with TCP, where retransmissions are typically done at the byte-stream level and can result in redundant data being resent.

QUIC also implements Probe Timeout (PTO) as part of its loss recovery mechanism. When no acknowledgments are received for a prolonged period, possibly due to heavy packet loss or network outages, QUIC's PTO timer triggers the transmission of probe packets to solicit an acknowledgment. These probe packets can contain retransmitted frames or simply act as heartbeats to confirm the connection's viability. If the receiver responds to the probe, the sender resumes normal operation; if not, the sender may escalate to connection termination or initiate other recovery procedures depending on the application's tolerance for loss and delay.

Congestion control is tightly coupled with QUIC's loss detection system. Upon detecting packet loss, QUIC's congestion control algorithm reduces the congestion window, limiting the rate at which new packets are sent to alleviate network congestion. However, because QUIC receives detailed feedback through its ACK frames, it can distinguish between isolated packet loss and more systemic congestion-related loss. This enables QUIC to make more adaptive congestion control decisions, improving both performance and fairness across competing flows on the same network path.

Another benefit of QUIC's loss recovery model is its synergy with encrypted transport metadata. In QUIC, packet numbers and other transport headers are encrypted, making it more difficult for middleboxes or attackers to infer network conditions based on visible transport-layer information. Despite this encryption, QUIC's loss detection remains robust due to the end-to-end nature of acknowledgment signaling. The sender and receiver collaborate directly, without relying on intermediary devices, reinforcing QUIC's privacy and security guarantees while maintaining high-performance loss recovery.

Loss detection in QUIC also benefits from its connection migration capabilities. When a device switches networks—such as moving from Wi-Fi to a mobile data connection—packet loss or reordering may occur during the transition. QUIC's ability to detect loss rapidly ensures that lost packets during a migration are promptly retransmitted on the new path, reducing disruptions for users and minimizing the performance penalty typically associated with network changes.

Because QUIC operates in user space, developers have the freedom to innovate on loss recovery strategies. For example, implementations can integrate machine learning models or network-specific heuristics to further refine how and when retransmissions occur. This flexibility allows QUIC to be tailored for diverse network environments, from high-speed data centers to high-latency satellite links, without being constrained by the limitations of kernel-bound protocols like TCP.

Ultimately, loss detection and recovery in QUIC exemplify the protocol's focus on responsiveness, efficiency, and adaptability. By combining packet-level granularity, selective acknowledgments, adaptive timers, and flexible retransmission strategies, QUIC delivers faster recovery from packet loss, minimizes unnecessary retransmissions, and ensures smoother application performance. These innovations are particularly valuable in today's mobile and wireless networks, where packet loss is common and connection stability is unpredictable. QUIC's approach ensures that users experience fewer stalls, faster recovery from disruptions, and more reliable services, regardless of the underlying network conditions.

Forward Error Correction: A Brief History

Forward Error Correction, commonly referred to as FEC, has long been a cornerstone in the field of communications, serving as a critical technique to enhance data reliability over noisy or lossy channels. The roots of FEC can be traced back to the early days of information theory, where the challenge of transmitting data accurately over unreliable networks first captured the attention of researchers and engineers. In the mid-20th century, as telecommunications expanded and technologies such as radio, satellite, and early computer networks emerged, the necessity for robust error correction mechanisms became increasingly apparent.

The foundation of FEC lies in the principle of adding redundant information to the original data before transmission. This redundancy allows the receiver to detect and correct certain types of errors without the need for retransmission. Unlike Automatic Repeat reQuest (ARQ) systems, where corrupted data is retransmitted after detection of an error, FEC enables the receiver to recover lost or damaged data on the fly. This characteristic makes FEC particularly useful in scenarios where retransmissions are costly or impractical, such as in real-time communications or in environments with high-latency links like satellite networks.

Claude Shannon, often regarded as the father of information theory, laid the groundwork for error correction with his seminal 1948 paper "A Mathematical Theory of Communication." In this work, Shannon introduced the concept of channel capacity and demonstrated that for any noisy communication channel, it is possible to achieve error-free transmission provided the rate of information is below a certain threshold and that sufficient error correction codes are applied. Although Shannon's theory did not specify how to construct such codes, it opened the door to decades of research that would eventually lead to practical FEC techniques.

In the decades following Shannon's breakthrough, various classes of FEC codes were developed, each suited to specific applications and network conditions. Early codes, such as Hamming codes, introduced the idea of detecting and correcting single-bit errors with a relatively small amount of redundancy. Hamming codes found widespread use in early computer memory systems, ensuring data integrity where single-bit errors could compromise entire operations.

As the demand for more powerful error correction grew, more advanced coding techniques were devised. In the 1960s and 1970s, Reed-Solomon codes gained prominence, particularly in storage and transmission systems that required burst error correction. Reed-Solomon codes could correct multiple adjacent errors within a block of data, making them ideal for media like CDs, DVDs, and digital television broadcasts. Their robustness and efficiency led to adoption in deep-space communications, where signals transmitted across vast distances were highly susceptible to interference and degradation.

The evolution of FEC continued with the development of convolutional codes and Viterbi decoding algorithms, which became widely used in early digital mobile communication standards and satellite communication systems. These codes processed data as a continuous stream rather than in blocks, enabling efficient error correction in real-time transmission scenarios. Later, turbo codes and Low-Density Parity-Check (LDPC) codes emerged as game-changing innovations, offering near-Shannon limit performance—meaning they could achieve error correction rates close to the theoretical maximum defined by Shannon's work.

LDPC codes, initially proposed by Robert Gallager in the early 1960s but largely overlooked at the time, resurfaced in the 1990s with the advent of more powerful computing resources. LDPC codes soon became integral to modern communication systems, including Wi-Fi, 5G cellular networks, and satellite internet. Their capacity to correct errors with relatively low overhead and computational complexity made them an attractive choice for next-generation networks that demanded both speed and reliability.

In parallel with these developments, the use of FEC expanded into the realm of packet-switched networks and real-time internet applications. Traditional TCP/IP networks typically relied on ARQ techniques, where packet loss would trigger retransmissions. However, as real-time applications like video streaming, VoIP, and online gaming became dominant, the inherent latency of retransmissions became a critical bottleneck. Here, FEC re-entered the picture as a method to supplement or even partially replace ARQ strategies, reducing the visible impact of packet loss on user experience.

QUIC, as a modern transport protocol, briefly explored FEC in its early iterations. Recognizing that many applications would benefit from built-in loss recovery mechanisms beyond traditional retransmissions, early drafts of QUIC included experimental FEC schemes. The goal was to reduce recovery times in scenarios with moderate packet loss, particularly in mobile and wireless environments where retransmissions could introduce unacceptable delays. By sending redundant recovery data alongside the primary data stream, QUIC aimed to improve the user experience for latency-sensitive applications, especially those involving real-time audio and video.

Although FEC was eventually removed from the core QUIC specification in favor of a leaner and more modular design, its exploration highlighted the ongoing relevance of FEC in modern protocol design. The challenge with integrating FEC into QUIC stemmed from the diversity of application needs and the variability of network conditions. A one-size-fits-all FEC implementation at the transport layer proved difficult to optimize for the wide range of applications QUIC serves. Nonetheless, the modular nature of QUIC allows for FEC to be implemented at the application layer or via extensions, giving developers the flexibility to tailor error correction strategies to their specific use cases.

Today, FEC remains a critical component of many systems that rely on QUIC and other transport protocols. Media streaming platforms, for example, often use application-layer FEC to ensure smooth playback despite occasional packet loss. Similarly, real-time communication tools incorporate FEC to preserve voice and video quality when network conditions deteriorate. The history of FEC, from early block codes to modern implementations in cutting-edge communication networks, underscores its enduring importance.

Forward Error Correction has evolved alongside the technologies it supports, adapting to the changing demands of telecommunications, computing, and now internet transport protocols like QUIC. While QUIC's core specification does not mandate FEC, its architecture reflects the lessons learned from decades of FEC development: efficiency, modularity, and adaptability are key to building resilient communication systems. FEC's rich history and continued relevance serve as a reminder that reliable data transmission, especially in an imperfect and unpredictable world, will always require innovative solutions at multiple layers of the network stack.

Encryption in Transit: QUIC Security Model

The security model of QUIC represents a bold and modern approach to securing data in transit, reflecting the increasing demands for privacy, integrity, and protection in a world where network traffic is constantly under scrutiny. From its inception, QUIC was designed to integrate encryption as a non-optional, default feature, making every QUIC connection secure by design. This marked a decisive shift from the traditional transport layer protocols like TCP, where encryption was layered on top, often as an optional configuration. QUIC merges transport and security in a way that enhances both performance and protection, fundamentally redefining what it means to secure data in transit.

At the heart of QUIC's security model is the mandatory use of TLS 1.3, the latest and most secure version of the Transport Layer Security protocol. Unlike TCP, where TLS is a separate layer that operates after the transport connection has been established, QUIC incorporates TLS 1.3 directly into the handshake process itself. This integration provides immediate encryption from the first packets exchanged, reducing the number of round trips required to secure a connection while ensuring that no data is transmitted in plaintext. In QUIC, encryption is not just a feature; it is a requirement embedded into the protocol's DNA.

The security model in QUIC operates across multiple dimensions, beginning with confidentiality. All QUIC packets, including those containing application data and most of the transport-layer metadata, are encrypted. The only parts of the packet header left unencrypted are minimal fields necessary for routing, such as the destination connection ID and a few flags to indicate the packet type. By encrypting packet numbers, stream identifiers, and other transport-level fields, QUIC mitigates a wide range of attacks that rely on analyzing unencrypted headers, such as traffic analysis, stream inference, or connection fingerprinting.

Integrity is another cornerstone of QUIC's security model. Every packet is authenticated, ensuring that any modification of data or headers during transit will be detected and cause the packet to be discarded. This is achieved through authenticated encryption with associated data (AEAD) ciphers, which combine encryption and authentication into a single step. By securing not only the payload but also critical parts of the header, QUIC ensures that packet tampering cannot occur without detection. This greatly reduces the risk of on-path attackers injecting malicious data or altering the behavior of the protocol during transmission.

One of the unique aspects of QUIC's security model is its ability to protect against replay attacks, a common threat in network security where an attacker retransmits captured packets to interfere with or disrupt a connection. QUIC incorporates protections against this by tightly coupling with TLS 1.3's built-in safeguards. The use of ephemeral keys, session resumption tokens with strict replay limits, and 0-RTT data restrictions all contribute to minimizing the risk of replay scenarios. When 0-RTT data is used, QUIC places strict limitations on how that data is handled, preventing state-changing requests or sensitive operations from being executed before full handshake completion.

Forward secrecy is another fundamental element provided by QUIC's adoption of TLS 1.3. Every QUIC session derives encryption keys from ephemeral Diffie-Hellman exchanges, ensuring that even if long-term secrets are compromised at a later date, previous communications remain secure. This is particularly important in a world where adversaries may store encrypted traffic for future decryption attempts.

Forward secrecy helps guarantee that such efforts will fail, as session keys are never reused and cannot be retroactively derived.

The mandatory encryption model in QUIC also provides privacy benefits that go beyond what traditional protocols can offer. Because QUIC encrypts more metadata than TCP+TLS stacks, it limits the information that can be extracted by passive observers or network intermediaries. For example, packet numbers in TCP are exposed in plaintext, allowing observers to infer flow control behavior, retransmissions, and other sensitive patterns. In QUIC, the encryption of packet numbers prevents this type of traffic analysis, making it harder to distinguish between different streams or applications based solely on packet timing and size.

QUIC's security model also includes protection mechanisms at the connection management level. Stateless resets, for instance, are crafted to be indistinguishable from valid QUIC packets, preventing attackers from easily detecting when a connection has been forcefully terminated by a server. Reset tokens, which are generated using server-side secrets, ensure that only legitimate servers can issue valid stateless resets, adding an additional layer of integrity and authenticity to connection closure mechanisms.

Another important feature in QUIC's security posture is its resistance to downgrade attacks. Downgrade attacks occur when an attacker forces two communicating parties to fall back to weaker encryption or older protocol versions, opening the door for exploitation. By requiring TLS 1.3 and encrypting version negotiation details, QUIC prevents attackers from manipulating the handshake to trick endpoints into using less secure configurations. This helps ensure that QUIC connections always operate at the highest available security standards.

The security model is further bolstered by QUIC's extensibility. As a user-space protocol, QUIC allows developers to quickly adopt new cryptographic algorithms and security practices without waiting for operating system-level updates. If vulnerabilities are discovered in existing cipher suites or if post-quantum cryptography becomes necessary, QUIC's modular design allows for rapid implementation of new secure algorithms without fundamentally altering the protocol's structure.

Moreover, QUIC's use of connection IDs plays a subtle but vital role in its security model. Connection IDs allow sessions to remain stable across network path changes, supporting mobility without compromising security. Because these connection IDs are opaque and encrypted within the transport header, they help prevent user tracking and fingerprinting across network boundaries, safeguarding user privacy during handoffs between networks such as Wi-Fi and cellular.

QUIC's security model also emphasizes the principle of minimizing reliance on network intermediaries. In traditional TCP deployments, middleboxes often inspect or modify traffic for purposes such as optimization or security enforcement. QUIC's encrypted headers reduce the role of such intermediaries, pushing responsibility for security and transport-layer behavior back to the endpoints. This restores the end-to-end integrity of connections and prevents unwanted interference from middleboxes that might inject RST packets, modify flow control signals, or disrupt session establishment.

In the broader context of internet security, QUIC represents a paradigm shift. It enforces a model where encryption is not optional, where metadata protection is prioritized, and where users' privacy and data integrity are built into the fabric of the transport layer itself. The lessons learned from decades of attacks on TCP and TLS are reflected in QUIC's design, offering a forward-looking solution that is resilient to the evolving threat landscape.

QUIC's security model does not operate in isolation but works hand-in-hand with its performance optimizations, including fast handshakes, multiplexed streams, and connection migration. By integrating security so tightly with its core features, QUIC ensures that users receive both high-performance and robust protection with every connection. The result is a transport protocol engineered not only to thrive in today's fast, mobile, and global internet but also to stand as a foundation for the secure communication systems of the future.

Middleboxes and Network Compatibility

The deployment of new transport protocols on the modern internet is complicated by the pervasive presence of middleboxes. These intermediary devices, which include firewalls, Network Address Translators (NATs), load balancers, and deep packet inspection (DPI) appliances, were originally introduced to enhance network security, manage traffic, and optimize performance. Over time, however, middleboxes became deeply entrenched in network infrastructure, creating what is known as protocol ossification—the phenomenon where network devices make assumptions about how protocols behave, making it difficult to deploy new ones. When QUIC was being designed, one of its biggest challenges was navigating the complex and often unpredictable landscape of middlebox behavior while ensuring compatibility across the diverse and fragmented internet ecosystem.

Middleboxes, by their nature, inspect, modify, and sometimes block traffic passing through them. For decades, these devices were engineered with protocols like TCP and UDP in mind, implementing hardcoded logic based on expected packet structures, header fields, and connection establishment patterns. TCP, with its well-defined three-way handshake and predictable sequence of control flags (SYN, ACK, FIN, RST), became deeply embedded in the behavior of these devices. Any deviation from these expected patterns could cause packets to be dropped, altered, or delayed. This legacy behavior created a hostile environment for the introduction of entirely new transport protocols, as middleboxes could interfere with or completely block unfamiliar traffic.

To address this reality, the designers of QUIC made a strategic decision to build the protocol on top of UDP. UDP, unlike TCP, is stateless and does not require a handshake at the transport layer. Middleboxes are generally more permissive of UDP traffic, often forwarding it without the deep inspection applied to TCP streams. By leveraging UDP as a substrate, QUIC sidestepped much of the ossification that had formed around TCP. This decision allowed QUIC packets to pass through most firewalls and NAT devices without triggering compatibility issues, giving it a better chance of widespread deployment.

However, using UDP introduced its own set of challenges. Many networks treat UDP traffic as lower priority compared to TCP, particularly in environments such as enterprise networks or public Wi-Fi hotspots. Some networks even block UDP entirely to prevent abuse, such as Distributed Denial-of-Service (DDoS) attacks that often exploit UDP's connectionless nature. Early QUIC deployments encountered these issues, with some users reporting that QUIC connections failed outright due to aggressive UDP blocking policies. To mitigate this, QUIC implementations were designed with graceful fallback mechanisms, allowing clients to revert to traditional TCP+TLS if QUIC could not be successfully established.

Middleboxes also presented hurdles related to packet inspection and manipulation. In the TCP ecosystem, middleboxes often terminate, split, or modify connections to enforce policies such as traffic shaping or intrusion prevention. Because TCP headers are sent in plaintext, middleboxes can inspect sequence numbers, window sizes, and flags to make traffic management decisions. QUIC, by contrast, encrypts most of its transport metadata, including packet numbers and frame types, leaving only a minimal set of unencrypted header fields for routing purposes. This encryption strategy protects user privacy and prevents interference but also means that middleboxes lose visibility into the transport-layer details they traditionally relied upon.

The encrypted nature of QUIC's transport headers limits the ability of legacy devices to optimize or throttle traffic based on flow-level information. While this is a win for end-to-end integrity and user privacy, it created friction with network operators accustomed to relying on middlebox-based traffic management. This forced a broader conversation about the evolving role of middleboxes in a world where transport-layer encryption is becoming the norm. Many operators began developing new network observability tools based on passive measurement techniques and endpoint cooperation rather than relying on deep packet inspection.

Despite these challenges, QUIC was designed with specific features to improve its compatibility with existing network infrastructure. For example, QUIC packets are padded during the handshake to resemble the size and structure of TLS handshake messages over TCP, helping to evade heuristics in middleboxes that might otherwise block unfamiliar traffic patterns. Additionally, QUIC incorporates version negotiation and retry mechanisms to work around NAT rebinding or IP address changes that can confuse legacy devices.

Another key compatibility consideration is related to NAT traversal. Because UDP does not establish a connection state at the transport layer, NAT devices often rely on activity within a short timeout window to maintain NAT bindings. If a QUIC connection is idle for too long, the NAT mapping may expire, causing future packets to be dropped. To address this, QUIC includes mechanisms like PING frames and keep-alive probes to maintain NAT bindings and ensure that connections remain viable over extended periods of inactivity.

In multipath and mobile scenarios, middleboxes can cause additional complexity by blocking or altering packets as devices move between networks, such as switching from Wi-Fi to cellular. QUIC addresses this through its connection ID abstraction. Instead of identifying a session solely by the 4-tuple of IP addresses and ports, QUIC uses opaque connection IDs that remain stable across network transitions. This allows clients and servers to continue a session without being tied to a particular path, providing resilience against NAT rebinding and route changes that might confuse traditional middleboxes.

As QUIC matured, its interaction with middleboxes sparked broader industry discussions about how transport protocols and network appliances should coexist in an increasingly encrypted internet. Some middleboxes have evolved to recognize QUIC traffic at a high level and treat it in a more application-agnostic manner, focusing on metrics such as connection duration, packet rates, and destination addresses rather than deep inspection of encrypted contents. Meanwhile, enterprises and service providers have begun rethinking traffic management strategies, shifting toward endpoint-based control where applications themselves signal quality-of-service needs to the network.

The relationship between QUIC and middleboxes ultimately reflects the growing tension between innovation at the transport layer and legacy assumptions hardcoded into network infrastructure. While middleboxes historically shaped protocol behavior by enforcing de facto standards through selective filtering and manipulation, QUIC represents a paradigm shift that challenges this model. By encrypting more of the transport layer, introducing flexible connection identifiers, and leveraging UDP to bypass TCP-specific ossification, QUIC enables a more agile and privacy-respecting internet.

QUIC's design acknowledges the complexity of global network infrastructure, offering a carefully crafted balance between compatibility and forward-looking features. Its ability to operate effectively despite the presence of unpredictable middlebox behaviors is one of the reasons it has seen rapid adoption by major platforms such as Google, Facebook, and Cloudflare. The lessons learned from QUIC's deployment highlight the importance of designing protocols that can thrive even within an internet shaped by legacy devices, while also paving the way for a future where innovation at the transport layer is no longer constrained by outdated assumptions.

Performance Metrics: QUIC vs. Legacy Protocols

Comparing QUIC to legacy protocols such as TCP reveals a significant leap in network performance that addresses the shortcomings of older designs while aligning with the needs of modern internet applications. QUIC's development was driven by the demand for faster, more resilient, and more secure transport-layer protocols, capable of meeting the challenges posed by today's latency-sensitive, mobile-centric, and content-heavy digital landscape. The performance metrics associated with QUIC consistently show meaningful improvements in areas such as connection establishment time, throughput, packet loss resilience, and overall user experience compared to traditional TCP-based stacks.

One of the most notable areas where QUIC outperforms legacy protocols is in connection establishment latency. Traditional TCP combined with TLS 1.2 typically requires at least two to three round trips to complete both the TCP handshake and the subsequent TLS handshake before encrypted application data can flow. This process introduces considerable latency, particularly in networks with high round-trip times such as mobile or satellite links. In contrast, QUIC, by integrating the transport handshake and TLS 1.3 handshake into a single process, reduces the time to first byte (TTFB) dramatically. For first-time connections, QUIC typically achieves secure data transmission in just one round trip, and in cases where session resumption is possible, it can achieve 0-RTT, allowing application data to be sent immediately. Empirical data from large-scale deployments, such as Google Search and YouTube, has shown that QUIC reduces TTFB by up to 20-40% compared to TCP+TLS, especially on high-latency networks.

Another key metric where QUIC shows a performance advantage is in its ability to mitigate head-of-line blocking at the transport layer. TCP enforces strict in-order delivery for all data, meaning that the loss of a single packet delays the delivery of all subsequent packets, even if those later packets have already arrived at the receiver. This behavior can severely degrade the performance of multiplexed applications like HTTP/2, where dozens or hundreds of streams may be sent over a single TCP connection. QUIC, by contrast, implements stream-level multiplexing directly at the transport layer, allowing independent streams to progress without waiting for others to complete. This results in lower latency and smoother resource loading in web applications. Real-world tests have demonstrated that QUIC reduces page load times by as much as 10-30% for users on lossy networks when compared to TCP-based HTTP/2.

Packet loss recovery is another dimension where QUIC demonstrates improved performance. In TCP, retransmissions occur at the connection level, and the protocol relies on cumulative acknowledgments and duplicate ACKs to infer loss, which can delay loss detection. QUIC, however, benefits from per-packet acknowledgments that include explicit acknowledgment ranges, enabling faster and more precise loss recovery. Additionally, QUIC retransmits individual frames, not entire packets, reducing redundancy and optimizing bandwidth usage. In mobile network conditions where packet loss rates tend to be higher, QUIC's enhanced loss recovery mechanism has been shown to reduce rebuffering events in video streaming applications by up to 15-20%, contributing to a more consistent user experience.

Throughput is another critical performance metric where QUIC competes strongly with legacy protocols. Because QUIC's congestion control operates in user space and supports modern algorithms like BBR, it adapts more rapidly to varying network conditions compared to TCP implementations, which are often constrained by kernel-level congestion control algorithms such as Cubic. QUIC's use of more modern and aggressive congestion control strategies enables it to achieve higher throughput on networks with large bandwidth-delay products, such as fiber-optic links and high-speed mobile networks. Studies comparing QUIC and TCP under controlled lab environments and real-world conditions have consistently shown QUIC achieving equal or higher throughput, particularly in scenarios involving high-latency or lossy links.

Connection migration is yet another performance-enhancing feature of QUIC that legacy protocols like TCP simply do not offer. TCP connections are bound to specific IP addresses and ports, making them brittle when network paths change, such as when a user switches from Wi-Fi to cellular data. Such transitions result in broken connections and require complete re-establishment of TCP and TLS sessions, adding latency and reducing application responsiveness. QUIC's use of connection IDs allows sessions to persist across network changes, preserving transport and encryption state and enabling seamless user experiences. This capability directly improves performance in mobile scenarios, reducing disruptions and connection downtime.

Security and performance are often seen as a tradeoff in legacy protocols, where adding encryption layers can increase overhead and latency. QUIC challenges this narrative by delivering mandatory encryption with TLS 1.3 while still outperforming traditional protocols in many performance metrics. The tight integration of transport and cryptographic handshakes reduces protocol overhead and streamlines session establishment. QUIC's efficient encryption of transport headers, including packet numbers and stream identifiers, provides both privacy and reduced exposure to network-based attacks without negatively impacting throughput or latency.

Another subtle but impactful performance gain comes from QUIC's packet structure. Because QUIC packets are self-contained and framed to carry multiple streams' data simultaneously, they make better use of available payload space. This efficient packing reduces the number of packets required to deliver application data, lowering transmission overhead and minimizing the impact of per-packet network fees in certain environments, such as satellite links or pay-per-packet mobile plans.

QUIC's improvements are also evident in its scalability for large-scale services. Data from Google and Cloudflare shows that QUIC reduces CPU utilization on servers by streamlining encryption operations and offloading some traditional kernel-level transport responsibilities to user space. This enables data centers to handle more concurrent connections with less resource strain, particularly when combined with optimized congestion control and multiplexing features.

While QUIC delivers significant improvements, it is important to recognize that performance gains can vary based on network conditions and deployment specifics. In well-provisioned, low-latency networks such as enterprise environments with reliable wired connections, the performance gap between QUIC and TCP may be narrower. However, as network conditions become more variable—such as in mobile or geographically distributed networks—the benefits of QUIC become increasingly pronounced.

Performance metrics collected across diverse industries have shown that services adopting QUIC see measurable improvements in user engagement, lower abandonment rates for media and e-commerce applications, and enhanced user satisfaction due to faster and more stable connections. These tangible benefits have contributed to the rapid adoption of QUIC and its designation as the foundation of HTTP/3, signaling a broader shift in the internet's transport-layer infrastructure.

The comparison of QUIC versus legacy protocols like TCP highlights more than just raw speed or bandwidth efficiency. It showcases a fundamental rethinking of transport design that better matches today's internet use cases. By addressing the limitations of older protocols while incorporating modern performance and security requirements, QUIC stands as a transport protocol built not only for current needs but for the evolving demands of tomorrow's internet applications.

QUIC's Impact on Web Latency

The introduction of QUIC has had a profound effect on reducing web latency, fundamentally reshaping the way web applications and services are delivered across the internet. Latency, or the delay between a user's action and the system's response, is a critical metric that directly impacts the quality of user experience. In the era of instantaneous access expectations, where users demand fast-loading pages and responsive web applications, high latency can be detrimental to engagement and satisfaction. QUIC was designed specifically to address many of the long-standing latency issues inherent in legacy transport protocols, and its deployment has consistently demonstrated significant reductions in both initial page load times and ongoing resource fetch times.

One of the most significant contributors to QUIC's ability to reduce web latency is its streamlined connection establishment process. Traditional web traffic using HTTP/2 over TCP and TLS 1.2 requires a minimum of two to three round trips to complete the transport and encryption handshakes before encrypted application data can be transmitted. This multi-step process adds valuable milliseconds or even seconds of delay, particularly in high-latency networks such as those found in mobile or geographically dispersed regions. QUIC, on the other hand, integrates the transport handshake with the TLS 1.3 handshake, reducing the setup to just one round trip for new connections and even achieving 0-RTT for resumed sessions. This means that web clients can begin sending encrypted HTTP/3 requests almost immediately, accelerating the time to first byte (TTFB) and enabling web pages to start loading faster.

QUIC's reduction of head-of-line blocking at the transport layer is another key factor in lowering web latency. In TCP-based systems, all streams within a connection are part of a single ordered byte stream. If a packet is lost, it prevents the delivery of all subsequent packets, causing delays even for independent HTTP requests. This phenomenon is particularly problematic in HTTP/2, where multiple streams are multiplexed over the same TCP connection but still share TCP's underlying packet ordering constraints. QUIC eliminates this issue by enabling true multiplexing at the transport layer, where each stream operates independently. If a packet loss occurs on one stream, it does not delay the delivery of other streams, allowing critical resources—such as CSS files or JavaScript required for rendering a page—to load promptly even if non-essential assets encounter loss or delay.

In practice, this improvement translates to smoother and more responsive web experiences, particularly on networks prone to packet loss, such as mobile or Wi-Fi connections. Studies by major web platforms like Google and Facebook have demonstrated that users on QUIC-enabled services experience faster page load times, especially in markets where network reliability varies. Users loading complex web applications with many concurrent resource requests benefit the most, as QUIC's transport-level multiplexing ensures that essential assets are not blocked behind lost or delayed packets.

Another element of QUIC's impact on web latency is its aggressive use of connection migration. As users move between networks—such as switching from home Wi-Fi to mobile data while browsing—a traditional TCP connection would be terminated and require re-establishment, incurring additional latency penalties. QUIC leverages connection IDs to maintain session continuity across IP address changes, preserving the active connection without requiring a new handshake. This seamless migration reduces disruptions for users who are browsing on the go or in environments where network conditions shift frequently. The reduction of downtime during these transitions directly improves the perceived speed and reliability of web applications.

Congestion control in QUIC also contributes to lower latency. QUIC's user-space implementation allows developers to deploy modern congestion control algorithms, such as BBR, which optimizes for low queue occupancy and high throughput. Traditional TCP algorithms like Cubic tend to prioritize throughput at the expense of latency, leading to bufferbloat and increased queuing delays. In contrast, QUIC implementations using BBR maintain shorter queues and respond more dynamically to available bandwidth, reducing the latency impact of congested network paths. This behavior is particularly valuable in shared network environments where multiple applications or devices compete for bandwidth, such as public Wi-Fi hotspots or corporate networks.

Additionally, QUIC's detailed acknowledgment frames enhance its ability to detect and recover from packet loss faster than TCP. The use of selective acknowledgments, along with the inclusion of acknowledgment delay information, allows senders to more accurately estimate round-trip times and detect network degradation sooner. This results in quicker retransmissions and adjustments to congestion windows, which, in turn, minimizes the time lost to recovery processes. Faster recovery means that resource loads and dynamic content updates within web applications happen more swiftly, improving user experience and keeping interactive applications responsive.

Another area where QUIC improves latency is in reducing protocol overhead. QUIC's packet structure allows for more efficient packing of data and control information within each packet, enabling applications to send the same amount of useful data with fewer packets compared to traditional TCP-based transports. This reduces the cumulative processing and queuing delays on intermediate network devices and helps minimize transmission costs, particularly in high-latency or high-loss environments.

The privacy and security benefits of QUIC also indirectly support its latency advantages. By encrypting transport metadata, QUIC prevents middleboxes from interfering with traffic in ways that often degrade performance. Legacy protocols like TCP suffer from network-based optimizations or interventions, such as traffic shaping or selective throttling based on visible sequence numbers and flags, which can introduce artificial delays. QUIC's encryption of packet numbers, stream identifiers, and flow control data limits these types of interferences, allowing connections to proceed with more predictable latency characteristics.

In large-scale deployments, QUIC's benefits are especially apparent when combined with Content Delivery Networks (CDNs) and edge computing strategies. Services that leverage QUIC and HTTP/3 to deliver content from edge servers close to end users can further reduce latency by minimizing both network distance and protocol overhead. CDNs deploying QUIC have reported significant gains in key metrics like TTFB, page load times, and user interaction times, with improvements ranging from 10% to over 30%, depending on network conditions and geographic location.

For end users, the impact of QUIC's latency improvements manifests as faster loading pages, smoother transitions between pages or states in web applications, and more fluid interactions in dynamic interfaces. E-commerce platforms, streaming services, and social media applications, where user retention is tightly correlated with responsiveness, have particularly benefited from these gains. Reduced latency not only improves the technical performance of a service but also drives higher engagement, longer session times, and increased customer satisfaction.

In the broader context of web evolution, QUIC's influence extends beyond mere technical efficiency. It reshapes the expectations for how quickly and reliably modern web services should operate, setting a new standard for user experience. As more browsers, operating systems, and services adopt QUIC and HTTP/3, the cumulative impact on web latency will continue to accelerate, further transforming the internet into a platform where speed, security, and resilience are inherently built into the underlying protocols.

QUIC Beyond HTTP/3

While QUIC is often associated with the acceleration of HTTP/3, its potential extends far beyond the realm of web browsing and traditional web applications. At its core, QUIC is a versatile transport protocol designed to solve broader challenges in modern networking. Its flexible, multiplexed, and secure-by-default architecture makes it a strong candidate for a variety of use cases that go well beyond HTTP/3, opening new opportunities for the evolution of internet protocols, cloud services, real-time applications, and emerging technologies that demand both high performance and resilience.

One of the most promising areas for QUIC beyond HTTP/3 is in the realm of real-time communications. Applications such as voice over IP (VoIP), video conferencing, online gaming, and interactive streaming platforms require low-latency, low-jitter, and highly resilient transport mechanisms. Traditional protocols like RTP over UDP, used in many real-time communication stacks, lack transport-layer encryption, multiplexing, and robust congestion control. By adopting QUIC as a transport layer for real-time media, developers can leverage its native encryption, fast connection establishment, and stream independence to deliver smoother and more secure communications. For example, voice and video streams in a video conference could each be mapped to distinct QUIC streams within a single connection, ensuring that transient packet loss affecting one stream does not impact the others.

QUIC's ability to facilitate efficient and resilient multiplexing makes it a suitable choice for replacing or augmenting other application-layer protocols beyond HTTP/3. Protocols like DNS over HTTPS (DoH) have already demonstrated the need for more secure and performant alternatives to legacy mechanisms. The advent of DNS over QUIC (DoQ) brings further enhancements to DNS privacy and performance. Traditional DNS queries are often subject to interception and manipulation, but by running DNS over QUIC, both queries and responses are encrypted and multiplexed over a single QUIC connection, reducing query times and protecting user privacy without the overhead of establishing new TCP or TLS sessions for each query.

QUIC is also finding use in transport scenarios for Internet of Things (IoT) devices and edge computing architectures. Many IoT environments operate in bandwidth-constrained or lossy networks, where minimizing overhead and maintaining session resilience are paramount. QUIC's lightweight handshake, reduced round-trip requirements, and connection migration capabilities make it particularly well-suited for IoT devices that may operate on unreliable wireless links or switch between networks as they move. Furthermore, its built-in security simplifies device management, as encrypted transport and integrity verification are guaranteed by the protocol itself, reducing the burden on application developers to implement bespoke security measures.

In the field of content delivery and streaming, QUIC's benefits extend beyond HTTP-based video services. As content delivery networks (CDNs) explore the possibility of using QUIC to optimize media delivery workflows, the potential to design application-specific transport protocols on top of QUIC emerges. For example, QUIC could serve as the foundation for custom protocols that optimize for adaptive bitrate streaming (ABR) or interactive video experiences. Since QUIC allows applications to control stream prioritization and flow control at a granular level, services could dynamically adjust transport behavior in real time, depending on current network conditions or user preferences.

QUIC's design also has important implications for cloud-native services and microservices architectures. In highly distributed systems, where microservices frequently communicate across data centers or between edge locations and cloud platforms, QUIC's reduced handshake overhead and multiplexing capabilities can improve the efficiency and speed of service-to-service communication. Service mesh implementations, which provide traffic routing, load balancing, and security features for microservices, could leverage QUIC to reduce the latency of inter-service calls while benefiting from its transport-layer encryption and stream isolation.

Emerging technologies such as augmented reality (AR) and virtual reality (VR) also stand to benefit from QUIC's strengths. These applications require ultra-low latency and high reliability to deliver seamless user experiences. In AR and VR environments, any delay in transporting data between clients and servers can result in motion sickness or a degraded sense of presence. By using QUIC to deliver critical assets like real-time scene updates, user interactions, and telemetry data, developers can reduce latency, minimize the impact of packet loss, and create more immersive and responsive experiences.

The financial services sector is another domain where QUIC is poised to make an impact. Trading platforms, fintech applications, and payment services all depend on fast, reliable, and secure communication between clients and servers. Traditional TCP-based systems often suffer from latency spikes during network congestion or transient packet loss. By shifting to QUIC, financial platforms can take advantage of reduced connection setup times, independent stream handling, and more adaptive congestion control, resulting in faster transaction processing and reduced risk of service degradation under load.

In addition to industry-specific use cases, QUIC's modular and extensible architecture supports the creation of entirely new transport protocols customized for specialized workloads. Because QUIC is implemented in user space, developers are free to experiment with transport-layer behaviors, congestion control algorithms, and stream management strategies without waiting for operating system-level updates. This flexibility opens the door to innovation in areas like distributed databases, remote desktop protocols, and even blockchain networks, where consistent latency and throughput can be critical to system performance.

Furthermore, QUIC's integration with future internet architectures is already being explored by standards bodies and research communities. As the concept of Information-Centric Networking (ICN) and next-generation internet designs gain traction, the modularity and security guarantees of QUIC make it a potential transport layer for experimental architectures that move beyond the traditional IP-based model. Its encrypted metadata, session migration, and extensible design align well with the privacy and efficiency goals of many of these forward-looking initiatives.

Another factor driving QUIC's expansion beyond HTTP/3 is the growing ubiquity of HTTP/3 support itself. As major browsers, operating systems, and cloud providers adopt QUIC as the underlying transport for HTTP/3, the groundwork is being laid for wider experimentation and adoption of QUIC in non-web scenarios. Libraries and development frameworks that natively support QUIC are enabling application developers to explore novel transport use cases while reaping the benefits of QUIC's performance, security, and adaptability.

Ultimately, QUIC's rise as a general-purpose transport protocol signals a shift in how developers and network architects think about application delivery and communication. Where TCP and UDP served as generic foundations for decades, QUIC introduces a modern alternative that prioritizes flexibility, encryption, and resilience at its core. Its use cases now extend well beyond accelerating web pages, touching every corner of the modern internet from real-time gaming and media to mission-critical financial systems and the emerging edge computing landscape. As QUIC continues to evolve, its influence is likely to expand further, establishing itself as a fundamental building block of the next-generation internet.

Streaming, Gaming, and Real-Time Applications

QUIC's architecture was designed to address the performance bottlenecks and limitations that have historically challenged streaming services, online gaming platforms, and real-time applications. These domains are highly sensitive to latency, jitter, and packet loss, and traditional protocols like TCP have often fallen short of delivering optimal performance under the dynamic conditions of modern networks. As consumer expectations evolve and the demand for low-latency, high-reliability services grows, QUIC has emerged as a transport protocol that not only accelerates web applications but also transforms the landscape for media streaming, multiplayer gaming, and interactive real-time communications.

In the realm of video and audio streaming, minimizing startup delays and avoiding playback interruptions are critical to maintaining user engagement. Legacy transport stacks that rely on TCP experience limitations due to TCP's strict in-order delivery and connection-level head-of-line blocking. A single lost packet in TCP can stall the delivery of subsequent packets, even if they belong to different segments of the video stream. QUIC addresses this limitation through its transport-layer multiplexing, where individual media chunks or segments can be transmitted over independent streams. This allows streaming clients to continue receiving other segments while recovery occurs for lost packets on a specific stream. As a result, video startup times are reduced, rebuffering events are minimized, and overall stream smoothness is enhanced.

Streaming services like YouTube and Netflix have started experimenting with and adopting QUIC to deliver content more efficiently to users across mobile, broadband, and wireless networks. QUIC's faster connection setup enables users to start playback with lower initial delays, while its stream prioritization features allow clients to prioritize key media chunks, such as video keyframes, over less critical data. Additionally, QUIC's advanced congestion control mechanisms, including support for algorithms like BBR, help streaming platforms adapt more dynamically to fluctuating network conditions, avoiding buffer underruns that cause video stalls.

Beyond video-on-demand, live streaming platforms such as Twitch, YouTube Live, and Facebook Live also benefit from QUIC's enhancements. Live streaming is particularly sensitive to latency, as reducing the delay between the broadcaster and viewers is essential for real-time interaction and engagement. QUIC's combination of faster handshakes, reduced transport overhead, and robust loss recovery ensures that live streams are delivered with lower end-to-end latency compared to TCP-based solutions. In crowded or lossy environments like public Wi-Fi or mobile networks, QUIC helps maintain stream quality without sacrificing viewer experience.

The gaming industry is another sector where QUIC's impact is being felt. Online multiplayer games require ultra-low latency to maintain competitive fairness and responsive player controls. Traditional TCP introduces latency penalties due to its retransmission and flow control mechanisms, which can disrupt gameplay with noticeable input lag or delay in game state updates. UDP-based game engines avoid some of these issues but at the cost of building custom reliability and congestion control systems at the application layer.

By leveraging QUIC, game developers gain access to a protocol that combines the best of both worlds. QUIC's transport-layer multiplexing ensures that critical game events, such as player movement or combat actions, are delivered over prioritized streams, while less time-sensitive data, such as background asset loading or cosmetic updates, can be assigned to lower-priority streams. This prioritization enables game engines to allocate bandwidth more effectively and reduce the likelihood of gameplay being affected by non-essential data transfers.

Moreover, QUIC's integrated encryption with TLS 1.3 provides built-in security for game communications, reducing the need for developers to implement separate encryption mechanisms. In multiplayer environments where cheating and data tampering are persistent concerns, QUIC's mandatory encryption and integrity checks offer an additional layer of protection. These features help safeguard both game servers and players from attacks such as packet injection, replay attacks, or session hijacking.

Real-time communications platforms, including VoIP services like Google Meet, Zoom, and Microsoft Teams, also stand to benefit from QUIC's innovations. Voice and video calls require consistent, low-latency packet delivery to ensure smooth and natural conversations. In traditional TCP-based implementations, packet loss or network jitter can introduce noticeable gaps in audio or visual glitches in video streams. While many real-time communications systems have historically used RTP over UDP to avoid TCP's drawbacks, they still require supplementary mechanisms to address congestion control and encryption.

By adopting QUIC as a transport layer, real-time communications platforms gain access to congestion control algorithms specifically tuned for interactive applications. For example, by adjusting congestion windows based on real-time feedback from acknowledgment frames, QUIC can better accommodate bursty traffic patterns common in voice and video communication. Additionally, QUIC's ability to perform connection migration enables ongoing calls to seamlessly continue as users move between different networks, such as switching from home Wi-Fi to mobile data, without experiencing dropped calls or audio cutouts.

QUIC also reduces the signaling overhead needed to establish new sessions, shortening call setup times and making real-time interactions feel more immediate. When combined with QUIC's transport-level multiplexing, real-time communication applications can separate audio, video, and control data into distinct streams. This ensures that packet loss affecting a low-priority stream, such as screen sharing, does not impact the delivery of more latency-sensitive streams, such as audio or video feeds.

Cloud gaming services, which require the continuous transmission of video frames and user inputs between data centers and end-user devices, further highlight QUIC's advantages. Services such as Google Stadia and NVIDIA GeForce Now depend on ultra-low latency and reliable packet delivery to offer responsive and immersive gaming experiences over the internet. The ability of QUIC to reduce handshake latency, mitigate transport-layer head-of-line blocking, and support flexible stream prioritization directly contributes to smoother gameplay and reduced input lag, which are vital for player satisfaction.

As network conditions evolve in real time, QUIC's congestion control and loss recovery capabilities help cloud gaming platforms maintain consistent frame delivery rates and minimize latency spikes caused by network congestion or packet drops. In competitive gaming scenarios, where milliseconds matter, this translates to more consistent and fair experiences for players, even on imperfect or variable network connections.

In addition to consumer-facing applications, QUIC is finding use in enterprise-level real-time applications, such as remote desktop services and virtual collaboration platforms. Remote desktop solutions that deliver interactive graphical environments over the internet must contend with latency and packet loss challenges similar to those faced by gaming and streaming services. QUIC enables these platforms to deliver high-fidelity user experiences by reducing round-trip times, maintaining session persistence across network changes, and improving responsiveness through its frame-based retransmission model.

Ultimately, streaming, gaming, and real-time applications share a common set of requirements: low latency, resilience to packet loss, seamless mobility, and efficient use of available bandwidth. QUIC's architecture was built with these exact needs in mind, making it an ideal transport layer for powering the next generation of highly interactive, media-rich applications. As adoption grows and developers continue to innovate on top of QUIC, its influence across these domains will only expand, enabling faster, more reliable, and more secure digital experiences for users around the world.

The IETF Standardization Journey

The journey of QUIC from an experimental transport protocol developed by Google to a widely accepted IETF standard is a story of technical evolution, community collaboration, and the persistent drive to modernize the internet's core infrastructure. As Google first introduced QUIC into its ecosystem in the early 2010s, it was clear that the protocol held the potential to revolutionize the way web and network applications communicate. However, for QUIC to move beyond Google's services and into the wider internet, it needed the legitimacy, scrutiny, and community consensus that only the standardization process within the Internet Engineering Task Force (IETF) could provide.

The IETF, known for its role in shaping critical protocols such as TCP/IP, HTTP, and TLS, became the natural forum for formalizing QUIC into an open standard. In 2016, Google submitted an initial draft of QUIC to the IETF, signaling its intention to transition the protocol from a proprietary solution to a globally accepted specification. The proposal sparked immediate interest from network engineers, browser vendors, infrastructure providers, and security researchers, all of whom recognized the transformative potential of QUIC but also saw the complexity of deploying a new transport layer in the ossified world of internet protocols.

The IETF's standardization process is inherently collaborative and iterative, involving multiple working groups and open participation from the global technical community. QUIC was assigned to the newly formed IETF QUIC Working Group, which quickly set out to refine and enhance Google's original design. While the core concepts of QUIC, such as its reliance on UDP, integrated TLS 1.3 encryption, and stream multiplexing, remained intact, the working group introduced numerous changes to broaden its applicability and address the concerns of stakeholders beyond Google's infrastructure.

One of the first major challenges tackled by the working group was the separation of transport and application layers. Google's initial QUIC implementation combined transport and HTTP semantics into a single protocol. The IETF, however, favored a modular design that would allow QUIC to serve as a general-purpose transport for more than just HTTP traffic. As a result, the working group decoupled HTTP from QUIC, creating a standalone transport protocol and defining HTTP/3 as a separate application-layer protocol that runs atop QUIC. This architectural decision greatly expanded QUIC's utility, enabling future applications beyond HTTP to leverage its performance and security benefits.

Another critical focus during the IETF process was security. While Google's early deployment of QUIC used a modified version of TLS, the working group aligned QUIC's cryptographic model with the standardized TLS 1.3 protocol. This ensured consistency with other secure internet protocols and made QUIC compatible with a wider array of security tools and compliance frameworks. Embedding TLS 1.3 into QUIC's transport layer also strengthened the protocol's defense against known attacks, reinforcing its position as a secure-by-default solution for modern internet traffic.

The working group also engaged in extensive discussions around loss recovery and congestion control. Given the diversity of network environments where QUIC could be deployed—from high-speed data centers to lossy mobile networks—there was a strong desire to ensure that QUIC's loss recovery mechanisms and congestion control were flexible and extensible. The resulting specifications allow implementers to choose or develop congestion control algorithms suited to their specific needs while maintaining interoperability at the protocol level.

One of the more subtle yet significant debates within the IETF centered on middlebox compatibility. Google's version of QUIC encountered issues with legacy network devices that interfered with or blocked UDP traffic. The working group took this into account, devising mechanisms such as version negotiation and retry packets to improve compatibility and ensure that QUIC connections could be established even in the presence of restrictive middleboxes. This middlebox-awareness extended to considerations around packet format, header encryption, and how QUIC's handshake mimicked familiar patterns to avoid triggering legacy network filters.

Over the course of several years and dozens of draft iterations, the IETF QUIC Working Group gathered input from a wide array of contributors, including major technology companies like Microsoft, Mozilla, Facebook, and Cloudflare, as well as independent researchers and engineers from academia and industry. The working group's collaborative model fostered healthy debate and consensus-building, balancing the interests of implementers, network operators, and end users.

Throughout the process, the working group also paid close attention to real-world deployment feedback. Companies that had already started deploying early versions of IETF QUIC in production, such as Google and Cloudflare, contributed performance data and operational insights, helping to inform refinements in areas such as packet pacing, stream prioritization, and connection migration.

Finally, in May 2021, after nearly five years of rigorous discussion and refinement, the IETF published QUIC as a series of RFCs (Request for Comments), marking the official standardization of the protocol. RFC 9000 defined the core QUIC transport protocol, while companion RFCs such as RFC 9001 and RFC 9002 addressed QUIC's TLS integration and loss detection and congestion control, respectively. Additionally, RFC 9114 defined HTTP/3, the version of HTTP designed to run atop QUIC.

The publication of these RFCs was more than a formal milestone. It represented the culmination of a community-driven effort to modernize the internet's transport layer, replacing the decades-old TCP stack with a protocol tailored for today's mobile, encrypted, and latency-sensitive applications. The standardization of QUIC validated its status as a global, interoperable solution ready to power web browsing, media streaming, online gaming, and countless other applications.

The IETF standardization journey also reaffirmed the importance of open collaboration in advancing internet technology. By opening the design of QUIC to scrutiny and input from the wider community, the working group ensured that the final protocol addressed the diverse needs of global stakeholders. The result is a robust, secure, and extensible transport protocol that is already reshaping the internet and will continue to do so for years to come.

With QUIC now firmly established as an IETF standard, the door is open for further innovation, including future extensions, alternative application protocols, and new congestion control algorithms, all built on top of the solid foundation laid by the collaborative efforts of the global internet engineering community.

The Drafts and RFC 9000

The path to RFC 9000, the official specification for QUIC, was marked by years of drafting, iteration, and refinement. The initial proposals that would eventually lead to RFC 9000 began as early drafts submitted by Google to the Internet Engineering Task Force (IETF) in 2016, based on Google's internal implementation of QUIC. This early version, already deployed at scale within Google's ecosystem, demonstrated substantial performance benefits compared to traditional TCP but also raised a number of questions about its general applicability across the open internet. The transition from a proprietary solution to a fully open and standardized protocol required extensive reworking and community collaboration, which came to define the drafting process.

The first series of IETF drafts retained many of the core concepts from Google's original protocol: multiplexing at the transport layer, native integration of encryption via TLS, and operation over UDP. However, to ensure QUIC would become a general-purpose transport protocol and not just a vehicle for HTTP traffic, the working group made significant changes early on. Google's initial version embedded HTTP/2-like semantics directly into the transport layer. The IETF decided to decouple the application and transport layers, resulting in a modular design where QUIC would function independently as a transport protocol, while HTTP/3 was specified separately as an application protocol that runs on top of QUIC.

Throughout the drafting process, compatibility with the broader internet ecosystem remained a critical challenge. Unlike Google's controlled infrastructure, where middleboxes and network paths were largely predictable, the open internet is filled with legacy devices and varied deployment environments that behave unpredictably with unfamiliar protocols. Several drafts focused on addressing these challenges by refining QUIC's handshake process, introducing retry packets to handle NAT rebinding, and formalizing version negotiation mechanisms that would allow clients and servers to gracefully fall back when encountering unsupported versions or restrictive network conditions.

Security also played a central role in the evolution of the drafts. Google's original design used a custom encryption scheme similar to TLS but tailored for QUIC's needs. However, the IETF's drafting process aligned QUIC's cryptographic foundation with standardized TLS 1.3. This decision ensured interoperability with existing cryptographic libraries, streamlined security auditing, and positioned QUIC as a strong candidate for sensitive applications that demanded robust encryption guarantees. TLS 1.3's incorporation into QUIC's transport handshake allowed for faster session establishment and forward secrecy by default.

The iterative nature of the IETF's drafting process meant that each draft cycle was subject to community feedback, which shaped the trajectory of the protocol. Researchers, engineers, and stakeholders from a diverse array of organizations provided input on congestion control, loss recovery, stream management, and transport parameter negotiation. Each draft brought refinements. For example, early drafts debated the specifics of packet number encoding and acknowledgment frame formats. These elements evolved to balance efficiency with clarity, with later drafts settling on more robust packet structures and flexible acknowledgment models that provided richer feedback for loss detection and congestion control.

By the time drafts reached the late twenties, QUIC had matured significantly. Discussions around stream prioritization, flow control, and connection migration were incorporated into the specifications, ensuring that QUIC would serve the diverse needs of modern applications, from web traffic to real-time communications. Additional mechanisms were added to facilitate stateless resets, which allow servers to terminate connections without maintaining connection-specific state—a key consideration for scalability and resilience in distributed systems.

Each new draft improved on the lessons learned from real-world deployments. Organizations such as Google, Cloudflare, and Facebook began testing draft versions of QUIC at scale, contributing operational data to inform the drafts. These deployments highlighted corner cases such as issues with NAT traversal, the need for connection ID rotation to enhance privacy, and the handling of packet amplification attacks. The working group responded by refining the retry and token mechanisms and introducing anti-amplification limits for servers when establishing new connections.

The final rounds of drafts saw consensus forming around the core features and mechanisms of QUIC. By this stage, QUIC's congestion control was formalized to support extensibility, allowing for algorithm experimentation while maintaining interoperability. Similarly, the handshake process was polished to support features like 0-RTT data transmission, enabling resumed sessions to send encrypted data immediately without waiting for the handshake to complete. This dramatically reduced the latency for applications where fast re-connection was critical, such as mobile users switching between networks.

In May 2021, after nearly five years of intense work, the QUIC protocol reached a major milestone with the publication of RFC 9000. This document formalized the QUIC transport protocol as an IETF standard, complemented by RFC 9001, which defined how QUIC integrates with TLS 1.3, and RFC 9002, which detailed the loss detection and congestion control algorithms recommended for QUIC implementations. These documents marked the culmination of dozens of drafts, hundreds of working group meetings, and countless technical discussions within the community.

RFC 9000 codified QUIC's core principles: a transport layer that eliminates head-of-line blocking through native stream multiplexing, encryption of almost all transport headers for privacy and security, reduced connection setup latency via integrated TLS 1.3 handshakes, and a design that is extensible to future innovations. The RFC emphasized how QUIC supports features such as connection migration using stable connection IDs, enabling sessions to persist as users roam between networks, and stateless reset mechanisms for efficient connection termination without retaining server-side state.

The publication of RFC 9000 did not mark the end of QUIC's evolution but rather its formal beginning as a standardized transport protocol ready for deployment at a global scale. With the specification finalized, browser vendors, infrastructure providers, and service operators could confidently invest in QUIC, leading to its rapid adoption across the modern internet. The release of RFC 9000 solidified QUIC's position as a successor to TCP in many applications, particularly those that value performance, resilience, and security.

The drafts that led to RFC 9000 exemplify how open collaboration and consensus-building can drive meaningful progress in internet architecture. The process was neither linear nor without disagreement, but it ultimately produced a protocol that reflects the collective wisdom and technical expertise of the global networking community. As QUIC continues to expand its influence across diverse applications and industries, the iterative drafting process and eventual publication of RFC 9000 stand as a testament to the value of standards bodies like the IETF in shaping the future of the internet.

The QUIC Working Group's Challenges

The IETF QUIC Working Group faced a wide array of challenges during the process of refining and standardizing QUIC into a globally deployable transport protocol. While QUIC began as a promising experimental technology within Google, transforming it into a flexible, open, and interoperable standard was a monumental task. The working group was tasked not only with enhancing and generalizing Google's initial design but also with addressing technical complexities, balancing competing interests from diverse stakeholders, and ensuring that QUIC would operate reliably across the complex and heterogeneous landscape of the modern internet.

One of the most immediate challenges the working group encountered was breaking free from QUIC's initial tight coupling with HTTP. Google's implementation had been highly optimized for HTTP traffic, embedding HTTP-specific assumptions directly into the transport layer. The IETF Working Group quickly realized that for QUIC to have broader applicability, it would need to become a general-purpose transport protocol decoupled from any specific application-layer protocol. This required rethinking how HTTP semantics would be layered on top of QUIC and eventually led to the creation of HTTP/3 as a distinct specification that operates above the QUIC transport layer.

Another significant hurdle was navigating the issue of middlebox compatibility. The internet is littered with firewalls, NAT devices, and other intermediary devices that are configured to expect well-understood behaviors from traditional protocols like TCP and UDP. The deployment of a fundamentally new transport protocol risked triggering incompatibilities, leading to dropped packets, failed connections, or degraded performance. The working group spent considerable time analyzing how QUIC packets could traverse these devices safely. They introduced mechanisms such as version negotiation, retry packets, and padding strategies to help QUIC traffic mimic more familiar UDP flows during the handshake phase, thereby reducing the likelihood of interference from legacy devices.

Security posed its own set of challenges. While Google's internal version of QUIC used a custom encryption scheme inspired by TLS, the working group needed to ensure that QUIC would align with established security best practices and regulatory requirements. This necessitated the integration of TLS 1.3 directly into the transport handshake, providing strong guarantees of confidentiality, integrity, and forward secrecy. However, embedding TLS into QUIC's transport layer required intricate engineering to merge two traditionally separate layers—transport and security—without introducing performance penalties or security vulnerabilities. Coordinating changes to QUIC's handshake while preserving TLS's state machine became a painstaking process that demanded close collaboration between security experts and transport engineers.

The balancing act between extensibility and ossification was another challenge that the working group continually faced. On one hand, the group wanted QUIC to be future-proof, allowing new features and extensions to be added over time. On the other hand, they had to ensure that middleboxes would not ossify around the first widely deployed version of the protocol, as had happened with TCP. To solve this, the group designed QUIC to encrypt most of its transport headers, hiding details like packet numbers and frame types from intermediary devices. While this reduced the risk of ossification, it also limited the visibility network operators traditionally had for diagnosing and managing transport-layer issues, sparking debates about observability versus privacy.

Interoperability across implementations also presented technical and logistical difficulties. Unlike TCP, where the operating system's network stack largely dictates protocol behavior, QUIC is implemented in user space, giving application developers flexibility but also introducing risks of fragmentation. With multiple organizations—including Google, Microsoft, Mozilla, Facebook, and Cloudflare—developing independent QUIC stacks, ensuring consistent interpretation of the specification became a priority. The working group coordinated a series of interoperability testing events, where engineers from different organizations would validate their implementations against one another in controlled environments. These tests revealed discrepancies, ambiguities in draft language, and implementation-specific bugs that were gradually ironed out over successive drafts.

Congestion control was another contentious topic. While QUIC's modularity allows for pluggable congestion control algorithms, the working group needed to define a baseline mechanism for loss detection and congestion management that would guarantee a level of interoperability and fairness on the network. Developing this baseline involved detailed discussions about algorithms, ranging from traditional loss-based methods like NewReno to more modern approaches such as Google's BBR. The final specification provided a recommended framework for loss detection and congestion control but left room for implementers to innovate, balancing the need for standardization with the benefits of flexibility.

The challenge of achieving consensus across a global and diverse group of stakeholders often extended beyond technical considerations. Commercial interests, differing deployment priorities, and varying network perspectives meant that discussions frequently involved trade-offs between competing goals. For example, browser vendors prioritized fast connection setup and minimal latency for web applications, while infrastructure providers focused on server efficiency, scalability, and operational simplicity. These discussions were further complicated by mobile operators, who raised concerns about battery consumption and radio resource utilization in mobile environments, where long-lived QUIC connections could influence power-saving strategies.

Throughout the process, the working group also had to remain vigilant about avoiding feature creep. The flexibility of QUIC tempted some contributors to propose non-essential features or complex extensions early in the standardization process. However, the group recognized that adding too many features at once could delay completion and jeopardize deployment. The decision was made to focus the initial RFCs on core functionality, deferring more advanced features to future extensions and later versions of the protocol.

The COVID-19 pandemic introduced another unexpected challenge as the working group transitioned to remote-only collaboration. The usual IETF meetings, which were traditionally held in-person several times a year, shifted to virtual formats. While online meetings allowed for broader global participation, they also prolonged debates, stretched timelines, and made it harder to resolve nuanced issues that benefit from face-to-face discussion and real-time consensus-building.

Despite these obstacles, the QUIC Working Group remained committed to an open, transparent, and consensus-driven process. The collaborative spirit of the group, combined with the shared understanding that QUIC had the potential to redefine transport-layer communications on the internet, kept progress steady. The group's ability to navigate technical, organizational, and social challenges ultimately enabled the publication of RFC 9000 and its companion documents.

The challenges faced by the QUIC Working Group underscore the complexities of modern protocol design. Creating a transport layer capable of serving the diverse needs of the global internet—while ensuring security, privacy, performance, and interoperability—is an enormous task. Yet, by embracing open collaboration and methodical problem-solving, the working group succeeded in delivering one of the most ambitious updates to internet transport protocols in decades. The lessons learned during the process will likely influence how future protocols are developed and standardized in the years to come.

QUIC's Modularity and Extensibility

One of the most forward-thinking aspects of QUIC is its inherent modularity and extensibility, qualities that differentiate it from legacy transport protocols like TCP. From its inception, QUIC was designed not as a rigid set of rules but as a flexible framework capable of evolving to meet the diverse and changing needs of modern internet applications. The modular nature of QUIC is deeply embedded in both its architecture and implementation philosophy, making it adaptable across a wide range of scenarios, from traditional web applications to emerging use cases like real-time media, gaming, IoT, and edge computing.

At its core, QUIC separates concerns in a way that promotes adaptability. The protocol defines a clear boundary between the transport layer and the application layer, allowing application protocols like HTTP/3 to operate on top of QUIC without being hardwired into its design. This approach contrasts sharply with early versions of QUIC, where transport and HTTP semantics were more tightly coupled. The IETF standardization process further enforced this modularity, ultimately positioning QUIC as a general-purpose transport protocol capable of supporting not only HTTP/3 but also other protocols such as DNS-over-QUIC (DoQ) and custom application-specific transport protocols.

A key feature of QUIC's modularity is its stream-based architecture. Unlike TCP, which delivers a single ordered byte stream, QUIC multiplexes multiple independent streams within a single connection. Each stream has its own flow control, error handling, and prioritization, giving applications the flexibility to tailor stream behavior based on specific needs. For example, in HTTP/3, streams can be prioritized to ensure that critical web assets load before less important resources like analytics scripts or background images. Similarly, in non-HTTP applications, streams can be mapped to distinct media tracks in a video conference or to different types of data flows in an online game.

The extensibility of QUIC is further enabled by its user-space implementation model. Because QUIC operates outside of the operating system kernel, developers can more easily experiment with and deploy new transport-level features without waiting for OS-level updates. This means that enhancements to congestion control, loss recovery algorithms, or stream management can be rolled out at the application level. The ability to iterate quickly and safely makes QUIC attractive to organizations looking to optimize transport behavior for their specific workloads. For instance, a real-time collaboration platform might implement a custom congestion control strategy tuned for interactive responsiveness, while a cloud storage service might prioritize throughput.

Another crucial element of QUIC's extensibility is its frame-based design. QUIC defines a variety of frame types that encapsulate different types of transport-level information, such as STREAM frames for data transmission, ACK frames for acknowledgments, and MAX_STREAM_DATA frames for flow control signaling. Importantly, the protocol allows for the introduction of new frame types without breaking backward compatibility. Receivers are required to safely ignore unknown frames, which means that experimental or future frame types can be deployed incrementally and without disrupting existing connections. This capability gives developers and protocol designers a pathway to innovate and extend QUIC's functionality while maintaining interoperability across different implementations.

Versioning is another aspect of QUIC's modularity that supports long-term extensibility. The protocol includes a built-in version negotiation mechanism that allows clients and servers to agree on a specific version of QUIC to use at the start of a connection. This system anticipates the evolution of QUIC over time, as newer versions may introduce changes to packet formats, handshake mechanisms, or transport behaviors. By embedding version negotiation into the handshake, QUIC creates a flexible platform where incremental improvements or even major protocol updates can be deployed without rendering older clients or servers obsolete.

Congestion control is an area where QUIC's extensibility truly shines. The protocol does not mandate a specific congestion control algorithm, leaving implementers free to select or design algorithms that best suit their use case. While the IETF recommends a baseline algorithm for interoperability—typically based on Reno or Cubic— many deployments, including those by Google, favor more modern algorithms like BBR, which optimize for bandwidth utilization and low latency. The modularity of QUIC's congestion control interface allows for experimentation with hybrid algorithms, application-aware congestion strategies, and network-specific optimizations, enabling performance improvements that were difficult to achieve under the constraints of TCP.

Security is another domain where QUIC's modularity has practical benefits. By tightly integrating TLS 1.3 into the transport layer, QUIC ensures strong encryption and forward secrecy by default. However, the modular design also allows for future cryptographic agility. Should new encryption algorithms or post-quantum cryptographic techniques become necessary, QUIC's handshake and key exchange mechanisms can be extended or modified without reengineering the entire protocol. This ability to evolve alongside the cryptographic landscape ensures that QUIC remains a secure transport protocol well into the future.

In addition to these technical aspects, QUIC's extensibility extends to its applicability across industries and application types. In the media industry, QUIC is being explored for adaptive bitrate streaming and low-latency video delivery. In the gaming sector, QUIC's stream independence and congestion control flexibility make it well-suited for synchronizing fast-paced multiplayer environments. In financial services, QUIC is being evaluated as a transport for latency-sensitive transaction systems that require both encryption and predictable performance. This versatility is made possible because the core protocol does not impose rigid usage patterns, but instead provides a flexible foundation on which domain-specific optimizations can be built.

The ability to extend QUIC through application-specific signaling is also noteworthy. Because the protocol allows applications to define custom frames and stream behaviors, developers can embed rich metadata or control information directly into transport-layer streams, reducing the need for additional signaling channels or out-of-band protocols. For example, a live-streaming platform might introduce custom frames to convey real-time quality-of-service feedback from clients to servers, allowing for dynamic bitrate adjustments at the transport layer itself.

Finally, QUIC's extensibility supports broader innovations in network architecture, including the growing use of edge computing and service mesh deployments. In edge environments, where applications demand ultra-low latency and high throughput at geographically distributed nodes, QUIC's ability to maintain persistent, multiplexed, and secure connections can significantly enhance service delivery. Likewise, service meshes can leverage QUIC as a transport foundation for east-west traffic between microservices, benefiting from its efficient multiplexing and security model while layering additional service-level intelligence on top.

QUIC's modularity and extensibility have helped redefine what modern transport protocols can achieve. It is not merely a replacement for TCP but a flexible platform designed for evolution. As internet applications become more complex and network conditions more dynamic, QUIC's adaptable framework ensures that it will continue to serve as a foundation for innovation across industries and technologies. Whether enabling faster web browsing, supporting real-time voice and video communication, or facilitating next-generation IoT deployments, QUIC's modular architecture positions it as a transport protocol ready for the diverse and evolving needs of the digital world.

Debugging and Instrumentation Tools

Debugging and instrumenting QUIC has introduced new challenges and required novel tools due to the protocol's modern design and heavy reliance on encryption. Traditional debugging techniques used for protocols like TCP or HTTP over TLS, where significant portions of transport-layer data and control information are available in plaintext, are largely ineffective when applied to QUIC. By design, QUIC encrypts most of its transport headers and all application data, protecting user privacy and security, but at the same time complicating the work of engineers tasked with troubleshooting, optimizing, and maintaining systems built on top of the protocol. To support these needs, the networking community has developed a variety of specialized tools and techniques that make it possible to monitor and debug QUIC traffic while respecting the integrity of its security model.

One of the first considerations when debugging QUIC is the protocol's end-to-end encryption. While TCP exposes headers such as sequence numbers, acknowledgment numbers, and window sizes to passive observers, QUIC encrypts critical transport fields like packet numbers and stream identifiers. As a result, traditional packet capture tools like Wireshark cannot directly interpret most of the QUIC-specific metadata unless additional information is provided. This has led to the development of decryption-assisted debugging workflows, where developers use key logging mechanisms to supply session secrets to analysis tools. For instance, when running tests or operating in controlled environments, engineers can configure their QUIC implementations to export TLS 1.3 session keys, which Wireshark can then use to decrypt QUIC traffic for inspection.

Wireshark itself has evolved to provide extensive support for QUIC, including the ability to parse and visualize QUIC frames, streams, and transport parameters when keys are available. This capability has proven invaluable for developers seeking to analyze stream-level behaviors, loss recovery dynamics, or congestion control responses within a QUIC connection. However, because production deployments must prioritize security, session key logging is typically reserved for non-production debugging scenarios to avoid exposing sensitive data.

In addition to packet capture tools, QUIC developers rely heavily on structured logging and tracing systems embedded within their implementations. QUIC's design encourages the generation of rich internal logs that provide insight into key transport events, such as packet transmissions, acknowledgments, retransmissions, congestion window adjustments, and stream-level operations. These logs are often formatted in JSON or other machine-readable structures, making them easy to ingest into centralized observability platforms.

One of the most widely adopted standards for this purpose is qlog, an open format developed alongside the IETF QUIC effort. qlog defines a standardized way to record QUIC connection events, enabling interoperability between different tools and implementations. A qlog trace typically captures events like packet sent, packet received, packet lost, stream started, stream closed, and congestion state changes, among others. By using qlog, developers and operators can generate detailed traces of QUIC sessions and analyze them using visualization tools such as qvis, which provides graphical representations of connection timelines, packet exchanges, and transport metrics.

Beyond protocol-level logging, applications built on top of QUIC also instrument higher-level behaviors, such as HTTP/3 request timings, stream prioritization decisions, and application-layer retries. By correlating these application metrics with qlog traces or packet captures, engineers gain a holistic view of how application logic interacts with QUIC's transport mechanisms. This multi-layered observability is crucial for diagnosing subtle performance bottlenecks or identifying mismatches between application expectations and transport behavior.

Another essential component of debugging QUIC is live telemetry and metrics collection. Many production deployments leverage instrumentation frameworks like Prometheus to collect real-time statistics on QUIC connections. Metrics such as round-trip time (RTT), congestion window size, retransmission rates, handshake success rates, and stream-level throughput are commonly exposed through monitoring dashboards. These metrics allow operators to quickly detect anomalies, such as increases in packet loss or unusual latency spikes, and to correlate transport-level trends with infrastructure events like server load, network congestion, or client-side issues.

For distributed systems and large-scale deployments, engineers also implement distributed tracing solutions that can follow individual user sessions across multiple services and infrastructure components. When combined with QUIC, distributed tracing provides valuable context on how specific network conditions impact user experience. For example, a trace might reveal that a particular QUIC session experienced a prolonged handshake due to excessive NAT traversal retries or that congestion control limited throughput during a peak traffic period, affecting video streaming quality.

The encrypted nature of QUIC necessitates close collaboration between client and server teams when debugging complex issues. Unlike TCP, where third-party network operators or security teams can often troubleshoot issues using passive network taps, QUIC's encrypted metadata means that meaningful insights usually require cooperation between both endpoints. Many organizations develop custom tooling that collects anonymized metrics directly from clients and servers to facilitate this collaboration, while still maintaining user privacy.

Developers also leverage unit tests and integration tests within their QUIC stacks to validate protocol behavior in controlled conditions. These tests often simulate adverse network conditions, such as packet loss, high latency, or reordering, to verify the correctness of congestion control responses, retransmission logic, and flow control mechanisms. QUIC's user-space implementation facilitates these efforts, allowing developers to emulate a wide variety of network conditions without requiring modifications to the underlying operating system.

Interoperability testing is another critical facet of debugging and improving QUIC. The IETF QUIC Working Group regularly organized interoperability events, often referred to as interop tests, where teams from different organizations tested their implementations against one another. These events uncovered edge cases, inconsistencies in interpreting the specification, and issues related to version negotiation or handshake behaviors. Insights gained from these tests have been instrumental in refining the protocol and resolving ambiguities in the RFC.

As QUIC evolves with new extensions and versions, debugging tools are being updated to accommodate additional features. For example, support for multipath QUIC (MP-QUIC) and future enhancements like forward error correction (FEC) extensions are gradually being incorporated into logging formats and analysis tools. Developers must continually adapt their instrumentation pipelines to capture metrics relevant to these evolving features, ensuring that performance and reliability remain transparent.

In summary, debugging and instrumenting QUIC requires a shift from traditional packet-based inspection to endpoint-centric observability, enhanced by standardized logging, live telemetry, and collaborative workflows. Despite the challenges introduced by encrypted transport headers, the networking community has successfully developed a robust ecosystem of tools to make QUIC's inner workings visible to engineers. These tools empower developers and operators to deliver the high-performance, low-latency, and secure experiences that modern users expect from applications built on top of QUIC.

Real-World Deployments: Success Stories

Since its inception, QUIC has demonstrated its potential to transform internet transport, and its success is perhaps best illustrated by its deployment across some of the world's largest and most demanding internet platforms. What began as an experimental project inside Google has now been embraced by a wide array of companies and industries, each leveraging QUIC to improve performance, security, and reliability in production environments. These real-world deployments provide tangible evidence of QUIC's impact, highlighting its ability to reduce latency, enhance user experience, and improve operational efficiency across diverse network conditions and application domains.

Google was the earliest adopter of QUIC, deploying the protocol at scale on its flagship services such as Google Search, Gmail, YouTube, and Google Drive. Given Google's deep involvement in both the creation and standardization of QUIC, it was natural for the company to take the lead in testing the protocol on a massive, global user base. Within months of deployment, Google reported measurable improvements in key performance indicators. For instance, YouTube users on mobile networks experienced fewer rebuffering events and lower startup latency when streaming video over QUIC compared to TCP. Google Search saw reduced time-to-first-byte and faster page load times, particularly in regions where network conditions were less stable, such as emerging markets with high packet loss rates or intermittent mobile coverage.

Facebook (now Meta) quickly followed suit, recognizing that QUIC's transport-layer improvements aligned well with the demands of its mobile-first user base. Meta deployed QUIC to optimize the delivery of content for its social media platforms, including Facebook and Instagram. The results were significant. Mobile users in regions with unreliable cellular connections experienced smoother scrolling, faster media loading, and reduced interruptions during video playback. For

Instagram in particular, the adoption of QUIC helped reduce the number of dropped connections and timeouts, leading to longer session times and improved engagement metrics. Meta's deployment also demonstrated QUIC's effectiveness at handling multimedia-heavy feeds, where multiple assets such as images, videos, and stories need to be loaded simultaneously. Thanks to QUIC's stream multiplexing, delays affecting one resource no longer blocked the delivery of others.

Another prominent success story comes from Cloudflare, a major content delivery network and security services provider. Cloudflare's early commitment to supporting IETF QUIC and HTTP/3 allowed thousands of websites under its protection to benefit from the protocol's features. By enabling QUIC at the edge, Cloudflare improved connection establishment times for millions of users worldwide. Independent performance tests indicated that websites served via Cloudflare over QUIC often experienced lower latency and higher resilience on congested or lossy networks. Cloudflare also reported operational benefits, including reduced CPU utilization on their servers due to QUIC's efficient stream and packet management, further showcasing how QUIC can reduce infrastructure costs while improving user-facing performance.

A key milestone in QUIC's journey was its integration into browsers like Google Chrome and Mozilla Firefox. By supporting QUIC and HTTP/3 out of the box, these browsers enabled end users to seamlessly benefit from the protocol's advantages without requiring manual configuration or updates. For Chrome, QUIC's integration was especially impactful on Android devices, where mobile networks are inherently variable. Users saw faster page loads, particularly on high-latency 4G and 3G networks, and improved browsing reliability in cases where network handoffs, such as switching from Wi-Fi to mobile data, would have otherwise disrupted TCP sessions.

E-commerce platforms have also realized benefits from QUIC. Shopify, a leading e-commerce infrastructure provider, experimented with QUIC to optimize storefront performance for its merchants. Online stores using QUIC experienced reduced cart abandonment rates, especially in regions where users connected via mobile devices on spotty networks. Faster page loads and smoother browsing during checkout flows contributed to an increase in completed purchases and improved overall user satisfaction.

In the realm of live-streaming, Twitch explored the adoption of QUIC to reduce latency and enhance viewer experience. Live broadcasts require minimizing end-to-end delays between streamers and their audiences. QUIC's ability to reduce handshake times and mitigate head-of-line blocking made it a natural fit for Twitch's low-latency streaming ambitions. By reducing stream startup delays and improving playback stability under variable network conditions, QUIC helped ensure that audiences experienced streams with fewer interruptions and closer-to-real-time interaction with broadcasters.

The gaming industry has also emerged as a beneficiary of QUIC's strengths. Riot Games, the developer behind the globally popular game League of Legends, has examined QUIC's potential to improve the responsiveness of its matchmaking and in-game services. While most fast-paced game traffic still relies on bespoke UDP-based transport for real-time gameplay, QUIC has proven valuable for background services such as player authentication, patching systems, and game store interactions. These auxiliary services benefit from QUIC's faster connection setup and encryption, reducing friction during key moments like logging in or accessing in-game content.

Telecommunications providers have similarly recognized the value of QUIC. Vodafone and other mobile carriers have conducted trials with QUIC to assess its impact on user experience across congested and high-latency cellular networks. The results were promising, with mobile subscribers experiencing faster loading times for web pages and video streams, even during periods of network congestion. These deployments revealed that QUIC's congestion control algorithms and stream independence helped networks maintain a higher quality of service without requiring changes to underlying mobile infrastructure.

Government and public sector services are also beginning to adopt QUIC. Websites for public health services, digital government portals, and educational platforms that have migrated to QUIC have reported reductions in latency and improved availability during traffic surges. During the COVID-19 pandemic, when demand for digital services skyrocketed, QUIC deployments helped ensure that users accessing critical information and services could do so quickly and reliably, even under network strain.

These success stories underscore the breadth of QUIC's applicability and the tangible performance gains it delivers across sectors. From high-traffic media platforms and real-time communication services to e-commerce and government portals, QUIC has consistently demonstrated its ability to deliver measurable improvements in speed, reliability, and user satisfaction. The protocol's success has been amplified by its ability to adapt to varying network conditions, its emphasis on security and privacy, and its compatibility with modern internet infrastructure.

The experiences of Google, Meta, Cloudflare, Twitch, and others have not only validated QUIC's design but also accelerated its adoption across the broader internet. With growing support from browsers, cloud providers, and application developers, QUIC continues to expand its footprint, shaping the performance standards for modern web and internet applications. Its success stories serve as a compelling argument for continued innovation at the transport layer, inspiring other industries and organizations to explore QUIC as a foundational technology for the next generation of connected services.

QUIC in Cloud and CDN Networks

The role of QUIC within cloud and content delivery network (CDN) infrastructures has become increasingly vital as modern internet services demand both speed and reliability at global scale. As more applications move into the cloud and edge computing paradigms expand, the deployment of QUIC across cloud environments and CDNs has emerged as a key enabler of lower-latency, more resilient, and more secure communication between clients, servers, and edge nodes. QUIC's architectural advantages, such as reduced handshake latency, connection migration, and native encryption, are highly compatible with the operational goals of cloud providers and CDN operators looking to optimize data delivery and improve user experience across diverse and distributed environments.

At the heart of the value proposition for QUIC in cloud and CDN networks is its ability to reduce connection setup times. In a traditional TCP + TLS 1.2 deployment, a connection requires multiple round trips before application data can be securely transmitted, which introduces delay, particularly in high-latency or geographically distant connections. Cloud environments are often distributed across multiple regions and zones, where users may connect to edge nodes that are hundreds or thousands of miles away. QUIC's integration of the TLS 1.3 handshake into the transport layer eliminates this delay, enabling a secure connection to be established in a single round trip, or even with zero round trips when session resumption is possible. For CDN operators, this means faster response times for web assets, videos, and APIs served from edge caches, leading to improved customer satisfaction.

The use of QUIC in CDN networks also addresses the persistent challenge of connection migration. Users today often move between networks—switching from Wi-Fi to 5G, for example—while interacting with cloud-hosted applications or media. Traditional TCP connections do not survive such network transitions without disruption, forcing clients to renegotiate new connections. In contrast, QUIC's use of connection identifiers (CIDs) decouples sessions from specific IP addresses, allowing a connection to persist across network changes without interruption. For CDN operators that manage distributed edge nodes and mobile user traffic, this capability ensures session continuity and reduces the likelihood of dropped connections during handoffs between network providers or physical locations.

Cloud providers are also increasingly leveraging QUIC to enhance backend service-to-service communication within distributed microservice architectures. Microservices, often deployed as part of large-scale cloud-native applications, require fast and secure communication to deliver responsive experiences to end users. QUIC's stream multiplexing allows multiple microservices to communicate efficiently over a single connection, with each logical stream operating independently. This reduces the overhead associated with managing multiple TCP connections and minimizes the risk of head-of-line blocking, which can impair the responsiveness of critical services. Additionally, QUIC's user-space implementation model allows cloud providers to quickly experiment with and deploy custom congestion control algorithms that better suit the performance characteristics of their infrastructure.

CDNs, by their very nature, are tasked with delivering content as close to the end user as possible. QUIC helps CDNs achieve this by facilitating fast and secure content delivery, even in challenging network conditions. For example, Cloudflare, a major CDN and security services provider, has reported significant reductions in latency for HTTP/3 (which operates over QUIC) compared to HTTP/2 over TCP. By operating at the edge using QUIC, CDN nodes can serve web pages, video streams, and API responses with faster connection establishment and improved resilience to packet loss, which is particularly beneficial in mobile-first markets and developing regions with higher network variability.

Security is another crucial factor driving the adoption of QUIC in cloud and CDN ecosystems. By encrypting most of its transport metadata and all application data, QUIC mitigates many security concerns associated with traditional protocols. CDNs and cloud providers, which handle sensitive customer data and application traffic, benefit from QUIC's default encryption model that integrates TLS 1.3 at the transport layer. This simplifies deployment and reduces attack surfaces, as the encryption of stream identifiers, packet numbers, and transport headers prevents common passive and active attacks, such as traffic analysis and packet injection.

Operational efficiency is another important consideration. Cloud and CDN operators often manage millions of concurrent connections, and TCP-based stacks can incur high CPU and memory overhead due to connection state management, retransmissions, and kernel-level limitations. QUIC's design offloads much of this work to user space, allowing operators to fine-tune performance through application-level optimizations. For instance, congestion control algorithms such as BBR can be implemented and adjusted on a per-application basis without waiting for updates to the underlying operating system. This flexibility is particularly valuable in cloud environments where heterogeneous workloads and varying network paths require adaptable transport behaviors.

The extensibility of QUIC also aligns well with the rapid innovation cycles typical of cloud services. Because QUIC supports the addition of new frame types and extensions without disrupting existing connections, cloud providers can experiment with features such as custom signaling, telemetry collection, or even multipath support to further optimize data delivery across diverse network conditions. The ability to evolve the protocol while maintaining backward compatibility is a major advantage for operators who need to deploy new features at scale while minimizing the risk of breaking client compatibility.

Beyond public-facing services, QUIC is being used in private cloud environments for internal workloads, particularly those involving APIs and backend services that require high-throughput and low-latency connections. Cloud providers like Google Cloud, AWS, and Microsoft Azure are exploring or deploying QUIC-based transports within service meshes and internal networking layers to reduce latency between microservices, improve efficiency under high load, and support emerging use cases such as edge computing and distributed AI workloads.

The proliferation of QUIC in cloud and CDN networks also has implications for monitoring and observability. Since QUIC encrypts much of its metadata, traditional network monitoring tools that rely on deep packet inspection or flow analysis must be supplemented with endpoint-based logging and metrics collection. CDN operators, for example, often deploy qlog-compatible instrumentation to capture transport-level metrics such as connection setup times, stream-level data transfer rates, and congestion control dynamics. By integrating these metrics into cloud-native observability platforms like Prometheus or Grafana, operators can maintain visibility into QUIC's behavior while respecting the protocol's privacy and security guarantees.

As QUIC adoption grows across cloud and CDN networks, it is also influencing business outcomes. Faster page load times, reduced buffering in video streams, and smoother API responses translate directly into improved customer satisfaction, higher engagement rates, and greater revenue for businesses that rely on cloud-hosted services or content delivery platforms. The ability to deliver services more efficiently and with greater reliability also reduces churn, particularly among users in mobile or bandwidth-constrained environments.

Ultimately, the deployment of QUIC in cloud and CDN infrastructures represents a shift toward a more modern, secure, and performance-oriented internet transport layer. It empowers providers to meet the demands of today's digital economy, where speed, reliability, and security are paramount. As edge computing, mobile connectivity, and content distribution continue to evolve, QUIC's role in shaping the future of cloud and CDN networks will only become more critical, driving innovation and enabling new possibilities across the global internet.

Edge Computing and QUIC Synergies

The convergence of edge computing and QUIC represents a powerful synergy that is transforming how data is processed, transmitted, and consumed across the modern internet. Edge computing aims to move computation, storage, and networking closer to end users and devices, reducing latency and alleviating congestion in centralized cloud infrastructures. QUIC, with its inherent design for low-latency, secure, and resilient transport, complements this shift by addressing the transport-level challenges associated with distributed edge architectures. Together, edge computing and QUIC create a framework for delivering faster, more reliable, and scalable services at the network's edge.

Edge computing seeks to solve the problem of high latency and bandwidth constraints by bringing compute resources physically closer to where data is generated and consumed. This decentralization reduces the round-trip times traditionally incurred when communicating with centralized data centers located hundreds or thousands of miles away. QUIC enhances this by minimizing transport-level handshake delays and optimizing data transfer across the edge nodes. Unlike TCP, which requires multiple round trips to establish a secure session when combined with TLS, QUIC completes both transport and security negotiations in a single round trip, and in some cases with zero round trips when using session resumption. This characteristic allows edge services to respond faster to user requests, enabling near real-time interactions in applications like streaming, IoT telemetry, and online gaming.

The modularity and stream multiplexing features of QUIC align well with the distributed nature of edge computing. Edge nodes often handle multiple services concurrently, such as content delivery, machine learning inference, and API gateways. QUIC's ability to multiplex multiple independent streams over a single connection allows edge nodes to handle these tasks more efficiently, reducing the need for multiple simultaneous connections and minimizing resource contention. By ensuring that loss or delay on one stream does not impact the others, QUIC ensures smoother delivery of critical and non-critical data alike. For example, in a smart city scenario, video surveillance streams, sensor data, and control signals can be transmitted over the same QUIC connection with prioritized handling based on application requirements.

The security model inherent to QUIC provides additional benefits when applied to edge environments. Edge nodes often operate in untrusted or semi-trusted locations, where the risk of man-in-the-middle attacks or traffic manipulation by intermediaries is heightened. QUIC addresses these risks by encrypting nearly all transport-layer information, including packet numbers and stream identifiers, providing privacy and integrity guarantees that are especially critical when edge nodes operate on public networks or third-party infrastructure. The encryption of transport headers prevents malicious actors from gaining insights into connection behavior or stream patterns, enhancing the confidentiality of data exchanged between edge nodes and end devices.

Another area where QUIC's synergies with edge computing are apparent is in connection migration and resilience to network changes. Edge deployments frequently serve mobile or roaming clients, such as connected vehicles, drones, or smartphones, which may move between different networks or change IP addresses during a session. QUIC's connection identifiers decouple the transport session from underlying network paths, allowing connections to seamlessly migrate across different network interfaces. This capability ensures session continuity even when clients switch from one edge node to another, or when failover mechanisms redirect traffic to alternate edge locations during outages or maintenance.

The user-space implementation of QUIC further complements the operational flexibility of edge computing. Since edge platforms often utilize containerized services or lightweight virtual machines, having a transport protocol that can be implemented and tuned at the application layer is a significant advantage. Developers can integrate QUIC directly into edge workloads, optimize congestion control algorithms based on localized network conditions, and deploy updates rapidly without needing kernel-level modifications. This agility allows edge deployments to experiment with novel transport features such as multipath QUIC (MP-QUIC), which could further enhance reliability and load balancing across multiple network links.

Edge computing environments also benefit from QUIC's efficiency in handling short-lived connections and high-churn traffic patterns. Many edge use cases, such as IoT devices or mobile applications, generate frequent but brief bursts of traffic. TCP's multi-round-trip handshake overhead can become a bottleneck in such scenarios, whereas QUIC's faster handshake and connection resumption mechanisms are better suited to the transactional nature of edge-driven interactions. For instance, a fleet of autonomous vehicles sending telemetry data to a roadside edge node can rapidly establish QUIC connections, transmit data securely, and move on to the next interaction without incurring the latency and resource penalties of traditional connection setups.

Furthermore, edge computing enables localized decision-making and data processing, reducing the need to backhaul large volumes of data to centralized cloud services. By pairing this with QUIC's stream-level flow control and loss recovery mechanisms, edge nodes can prioritize time-sensitive data while still ensuring reliable delivery of bulk data when needed. This is particularly valuable for use cases like video analytics at the edge, where real-time alerts can be sent with higher priority, while non-urgent archival footage is transmitted in the background over lower-priority streams.

The synergy between QUIC and edge computing extends into sectors like healthcare, manufacturing, and retail, where edge nodes increasingly power mission-critical applications. In a hospital environment, edge nodes can facilitate telemedicine sessions, manage patient monitoring devices, and process medical imaging closer to the point of care. QUIC ensures that these latency-sensitive applications perform reliably and securely, even when the hospital's network conditions are less than ideal. Similarly, in retail environments, edge nodes can power in-store analytics, digital signage, and point-of-sale systems, while QUIC optimizes data transfer between customer devices, store infrastructure, and the cloud.

Additionally, QUIC plays a role in enabling real-time collaboration at the edge. In environments where remote teams access shared resources hosted at edge locations, such as collaborative design platforms or edge-hosted development environments, QUIC enhances responsiveness and security. Its multiplexing capabilities allow multiple simultaneous interactions—like file transfers, chat messages, and screen sharing—to coexist within a single, encrypted transport session, reducing overhead and improving perceived application performance.

As the demand for distributed services grows, the combination of edge computing and QUIC is setting new benchmarks for latency, reliability, and operational efficiency. The two technologies complement each other, with QUIC acting as an enabler that allows edge nodes to meet modern user expectations for seamless, fast, and secure digital experiences. Edge nodes empowered by QUIC can deliver content and services that are highly resilient to fluctuating network conditions, while maintaining the scalability and privacy essential to modern applications.

In short, the collaboration between QUIC and edge computing addresses the modern internet's shift away from centralized models towards more dynamic, distributed systems. The ongoing evolution of both technologies will likely lead to further innovation, shaping the future of how applications are architected, deployed, and consumed on a truly global scale.

Privacy and Anonymity Considerations

As modern internet users grow increasingly concerned with the privacy of their online activities and the potential for surveillance, the design of QUIC introduces a new layer of protection against common privacy threats present in older transport protocols. The traditional TCP + TLS stack leaves much of its metadata exposed in plaintext, enabling network intermediaries and adversaries to gather information about communication patterns, traffic characteristics, and user behaviors. QUIC, by encrypting nearly all of its transport-layer metadata, represents a significant shift toward more privacy-conscious transport-layer protocols. However, while QUIC's design greatly improves user privacy in several key areas, it also introduces new considerations and trade-offs that must be carefully examined by both protocol designers and implementers.

One of the most important privacy-enhancing features of QUIC is its encryption of packet numbers and transport headers. In TCP, critical fields such as sequence numbers, acknowledgment numbers, window sizes, and flags are all visible to any on-path observer. This exposure allows passive entities, such as ISPs or state actors, to build detailed profiles of user activities by analyzing patterns in TCP flows. By encrypting the packet number and stream-related metadata, QUIC thwarts many of these passive surveillance techniques. Observers can no longer easily infer information such as how many streams are multiplexed within a connection, when packets are retransmitted, or how many packets are lost and recovered, all of which previously served as indirect signals about user activities or application behaviors.

Furthermore, QUIC's encryption of transport metadata complicates traffic analysis attacks, which aim to deduce information from traffic timing, sizes, and flow characteristics. While QUIC cannot fully eliminate traffic analysis risks—since packet sizes and timing remain observable to some extent—it does limit the granularity of information exposed to network intermediaries. For example, an attacker cannot tell whether a stream carries HTTP requests, media data, or other types of application content because stream identifiers and frame types are encrypted. This obfuscation enhances user privacy by making QUIC flows more opaque to entities attempting to infer sensitive data from visible transport-layer signals.

The use of connection IDs (CIDs) in QUIC further supports privacy goals, particularly in mobile environments. Unlike TCP connections, which are bound to a specific 4-tuple of IP addresses and ports, QUIC employs opaque connection IDs that remain stable even when the underlying network path changes. This feature enables seamless connection migration, but it also protects user privacy by preventing network intermediaries from trivially correlating connections across different IP addresses or network transitions. Since CIDs are designed to be unpredictable and non-identifying, they hinder tracking techniques that rely on monitoring persistent network-level identifiers over time.

Despite these advances, QUIC's reliance on connection IDs introduces subtle privacy considerations of its own. Improperly designed CID schemes could inadvertently expose information about a client's connection to different parties. For instance, if a server's CID encoding includes identifiable information about the backend infrastructure or user-specific data, this could enable linkability between sessions or reveal details about a user's path through a content delivery network (CDN) or cloud provider's infrastructure. To address this risk, the QUIC specification encourages implementations to use randomized, opaque CIDs and to rotate them as needed to minimize linkability and fingerprinting opportunities.

QUIC's approach to encryption also has implications for anonymity in adversarial environments. In regions where network operators or governments deploy pervasive deep packet inspection (DPI) tools, QUIC's encryption of transport-layer headers makes it harder for these entities to distinguish between different types of traffic. However, QUIC's handshake remains visible in plaintext due to its reliance on the TLS 1.3 handshake, which exposes a small set of metadata, such as the server name indication (SNI) and transport parameters. The exposure of SNI, in particular, is a long-standing issue in TLS that has privacy implications for users attempting to access sensitive or censored content, as it allows adversaries to identify the destination service even when the payload itself is encrypted.

To mitigate this, efforts such as Encrypted Client Hello (ECH) are being pursued by the IETF to encrypt the SNI and other handshake metadata, further strengthening QUIC's privacy posture. Once ECH is widely deployed, QUIC connections will become even more resistant to traffic classification and censorship, offering users improved anonymity when accessing online services in hostile environments.

It is also worth noting that QUIC's end-to-end encryption model reduces the influence of middleboxes, such as caching proxies, that often intercept and modify traffic in traditional TCP-based deployments. While this enhances user privacy by limiting third-party interference, it also creates tension with some network operators who have historically relied on middlebox visibility for network management, traffic optimization, or policy enforcement. The reduced observability into transport-layer details forces a paradigm shift, where traffic engineering and security controls must be implemented at the endpoints or rely on aggregate metrics rather than packet-level inspection.

An additional layer of complexity comes from the fact that QUIC's improved privacy properties may be leveraged by malicious actors as well. Attackers can use QUIC to obfuscate command-and-control (C2) channels or data exfiltration streams in the same way that legitimate users rely on it to protect sensitive information. This dual-use nature of privacy-enhancing technologies necessitates careful consideration by security teams, who must develop new detection and mitigation strategies that respect user privacy while defending against abuse.

In terms of user anonymity, QUIC's improvements should be viewed as one piece of a larger puzzle. While the protocol enhances transport-layer privacy, users seeking full anonymity—such as whistleblowers or activists operating under oppressive regimes—must still rely on anonymity networks like Tor, which implement additional protections against IP address leakage, timing correlation attacks, and sophisticated traffic analysis. QUIC's encryption does, however, complement such systems by reducing metadata exposure during transport.

Developers building applications on top of QUIC must also consider the privacy implications of their specific use cases. Even with QUIC's transport-layer protections, application-layer metadata—such as HTTP headers, cookies, or query parameters—may still reveal sensitive information if not properly secured. Best practices such as minimizing metadata, adopting encrypted DNS (e.g., DoH or DoQ), and implementing application-layer encryption where necessary are essential to maximize the privacy benefits provided by QUIC.

Ultimately, QUIC reflects a deliberate shift toward privacy-by-design principles at the transport layer. By encrypting more metadata, limiting linkability, and supporting future enhancements like ECH, QUIC offers a significantly stronger privacy model than its predecessors. However, these advances must be combined with thoughtful implementation choices and complementary privacy-preserving technologies to deliver holistic protection for users navigating today's increasingly monitored and data-driven internet.

The Future of Transport Protocols

The evolution of transport protocols has always been driven by the relentless demand for faster, more secure, and more reliable communication across increasingly complex and global networks. As digital ecosystems continue to expand and diversify, the future of transport protocols will be shaped by trends such as ubiquitous encryption, edge computing, decentralized architectures, and the growing dominance of real-time applications. The emergence of QUIC marked a pivotal moment in this journey, but it is also a signpost pointing toward the next generation of transport protocols that will define the internet's future.

One of the defining characteristics of future transport protocols is the continued prioritization of encryption and privacy at the transport layer. QUIC's success has demonstrated that it is possible to integrate encryption directly into transport protocols without sacrificing performance. This sets a precedent for future designs, where confidentiality and integrity will no longer be optional or relegated to higher layers like TLS but instead be deeply embedded into transport mechanisms. As concerns over surveillance, data breaches, and privacy violations grow, future transport protocols will likely expand on this by supporting post-quantum cryptography and more sophisticated forms of metadata obfuscation to resist even the most advanced traffic analysis techniques.

Performance optimization will remain another critical focus area. The need for low-latency, high-throughput connections is growing as immersive applications such as augmented reality (AR), virtual reality (VR), and cloud gaming become more mainstream. These applications place stringent requirements on transport layers to deliver ultra-responsive communication, even under conditions of network variability, congestion, or packet loss. The future transport protocols will likely incorporate multipath capabilities by default, enabling simultaneous use of multiple network paths, such as Wi-Fi and 5G, to increase reliability and optimize latency dynamically. The exploration of multipath QUIC (MP-QUIC) is an example of how protocols are evolving in this direction, with research suggesting that multipath support can significantly improve resilience and performance in mobile and edge scenarios.

Another trend shaping the future of transport protocols is programmability and adaptability. Whereas traditional protocols like TCP are tightly integrated into operating system kernels, limiting flexibility, modern and future transport protocols will increasingly operate in user space. This shift allows for rapid iteration, experimentation with congestion control algorithms, and application-specific transport optimizations. Developers will have the ability to fine-tune transport behaviors based on the needs of their specific applications or environments, whether that means optimizing for latency-sensitive interactive media or for high-throughput data replication between data centers.

Decentralization will also play a major role in influencing transport protocol design. As blockchain networks, peer-to-peer applications, and distributed ledgers become more common, transport protocols will need to accommodate the requirements of decentralized systems. These environments often feature unpredictable node availability, high churn rates, and the absence of centralized authority. Future transport protocols will need to support seamless peer discovery, NAT traversal, and adaptive routing mechanisms that enable stable communication in decentralized settings. Emerging work on peer-to-peer adaptations of QUIC and other next-generation transports reflects the growing importance of supporting decentralized internet infrastructures.

The integration of artificial intelligence and machine learning into transport-layer decision-making is another frontier likely to influence future protocols. By leveraging real-time telemetry and predictive analytics, transport protocols will be able to adapt dynamically to network conditions, application demands, and user behaviors. AI-driven congestion control, loss recovery, and stream prioritization could lead to significant improvements in user experience, particularly in environments with highly variable bandwidth or unpredictable traffic patterns. For instance, transport layers could automatically adjust parameters to minimize video buffering during live streaming or to reduce latency spikes during online gaming sessions.

Edge computing will also drive innovation at the transport layer. As more compute resources shift closer to end users, transport protocols must adapt to facilitate ultra-low-latency communication between edge nodes and client devices. This will involve optimizing for localized data flows, supporting persistent connections that span dynamic and heterogeneous network topologies, and enhancing session mobility across distributed edge locations. The connection migration features pioneered by QUIC will serve as a blueprint, but future protocols may expand on these capabilities to include session handoffs between edge clusters, predictive path selection, and localized congestion management.

Standardization efforts will continue to be critical as new transport protocols emerge. One of the key lessons from the deployment of QUIC is that wide-scale interoperability requires open collaboration and consensus-building across industries, academia, and the broader internet community. The IETF will likely remain a central body in this process, ensuring that future transport protocols are designed with security, scalability, and fairness in mind. Standardization will also facilitate the development of common debugging, monitoring, and observability tools that allow operators to manage transport-layer behaviors despite the increasing use of encryption and metadata protection.

Security considerations will grow more complex as transport protocols evolve. While encrypting transport metadata enhances privacy, it also challenges traditional network defense mechanisms that rely on packet inspection and flow analysis. As a result, future transport protocols will likely include built-in security features such as end-to-end integrity checks, abuse detection signals, and mechanisms to balance user privacy with network operator visibility. Emerging technologies like Encrypted Client Hello (ECH) and privacy-preserving traffic measurement frameworks will influence how future protocols manage this delicate balance.

The evolution of transport protocols will also respond to the increasing need for energy efficiency and sustainability in network operations. As data centers and edge nodes scale to meet global demand, optimizing transport-layer behavior to minimize CPU usage, reduce retransmissions, and improve overall bandwidth efficiency will become an environmental imperative. Energy-aware transport algorithms that intelligently modulate packet rates, connection lifetimes, and stream prioritization based on resource availability could become standard features in next-generation protocols.

Finally, future transport protocols will need to be resilient by design. As cyber threats continue to evolve and internet infrastructure becomes more decentralized and diverse, protocols must be designed to withstand a wide variety of attacks, from denial-of-service attempts to state exhaustion and side-channel exploits. Leveraging concepts like stateless resets, connection migration, and adaptive congestion control will be crucial to ensuring that transport protocols remain robust under adverse conditions.

Ultimately, the trajectory set by QUIC is a clear indicator of where transport protocols are headed: towards a future defined by modularity, security, agility, and adaptability. As applications grow more demanding and network environments become more dynamic, the need for transport protocols that can evolve in step with these changes will only become more pressing. The future of transport protocols lies in their ability to bridge the growing complexity of the modern internet while delivering the speed, reliability, and privacy that users and services demand. This next chapter will be shaped by a collective effort to innovate beyond the limitations of legacy designs and to create a transport layer that is truly built for the future of digital communication.

The Role of QUIC in IoT and 5G

The rapid growth of the Internet of Things (IoT) and the global rollout of 5G networks are reshaping the future of connectivity. Both technologies are driving unprecedented demands on transport protocols to deliver low-latency, secure, and efficient communication across diverse and often resource-constrained environments. QUIC, with its modern architecture and performance-focused design, is well-positioned to play a transformative role in supporting the evolving needs of IoT and 5G ecosystems. As billions of devices come online and networks become more heterogeneous, QUIC's features align closely with the requirements of these interconnected worlds.

In the IoT landscape, devices often operate under conditions where bandwidth is limited, power consumption is critical, and network reliability can be inconsistent. Traditional transport protocols like TCP, with their multi-round-trip connection establishment and head-of-line blocking, present significant inefficiencies in these environments. QUIC, in contrast, reduces handshake overhead by combining transport and encryption negotiation into a single round trip. In cases where session resumption is available, it can even achieve zero round-trip communication. This capability significantly lowers the time and energy needed to establish secure sessions, which is particularly advantageous for battery-powered IoT devices that frequently wake from sleep states to transmit small bursts of data before returning to low-power modes.

QUIC's native encryption, via mandatory TLS 1.3 integration, ensures that IoT data is protected in transit. Given the sensitive nature of many IoT deployments—ranging from smart home devices to industrial control systems—securing communications is paramount. By encrypting both application data and most transport-layer metadata, QUIC offers end-to-end confidentiality and integrity for IoT traffic. Furthermore, because QUIC encrypts its transport headers, it helps shield IoT communications from passive monitoring and network-based attacks, which are common threats in environments with widespread device deployments.

Another key advantage of QUIC in IoT contexts is its stream multiplexing capability. Many IoT devices are tasked with handling

139

multiple types of data simultaneously, such as sensor readings, firmware updates, and telemetry reports. QUIC enables these different data streams to be sent independently over a single connection, avoiding the head-of-line blocking issues that can occur with TCP. This multiplexing allows for more efficient use of bandwidth and ensures that critical data, such as security alerts or real-time sensor readings, are not delayed by less urgent transmissions like background updates.

The rise of 5G networks brings additional dimensions where QUIC's design excels. 5G promises ultra-low latency, higher throughput, and support for massive numbers of simultaneously connected devices, making it a catalyst for advanced IoT applications such as autonomous vehicles, remote surgery, and smart city infrastructures. However, to fully realize these benefits, the underlying transport protocols must be capable of adapting to 5G's dynamic and high-performance environment. QUIC's ability to operate effectively in variable network conditions—such as when devices transition between different types of 5G cells or between 5G and Wi-Fi networks—is critical for maintaining session continuity and reducing interruptions.

One of QUIC's standout features in this regard is connection migration. In mobile scenarios, including those powered by 5G, devices frequently change IP addresses as they move between networks or when network paths are rerouted due to congestion or signal degradation. Unlike TCP, which is tightly coupled to a specific IP address and port combination, QUIC's use of connection identifiers allows sessions to persist across such changes without requiring a full re-establishment of the connection. This feature is essential for supporting seamless mobility in 5G-powered IoT devices, where maintaining low-latency, uninterrupted communication streams is crucial.

In dense 5G environments, where thousands of IoT devices may be connected to the same base station or edge node, congestion control and efficient resource utilization become critical challenges. QUIC's congestion control mechanisms are modular and can be tuned to the specific characteristics of 5G networks. For example, congestion control algorithms such as BBR, which are optimized for minimizing bufferbloat and maintaining high throughput, can be deployed in QUIC implementations to better utilize the high-capacity links provided by 5G infrastructure. This adaptability helps ensure that IoT devices can maintain consistent performance, even in scenarios with variable network loads or fluctuating link quality.

Furthermore, 5G's emphasis on edge computing—bringing compute and storage resources closer to end devices—aligns well with QUIC's strengths. By reducing the distance between IoT devices and their data processing nodes, edge computing helps lower latency and offloads traffic from core networks. QUIC enhances this by facilitating fast and secure transport between devices and edge nodes, ensuring that time-sensitive IoT applications, such as vehicle-to-infrastructure (V2I) communications or industrial automation systems, can exchange data with minimal delay and high reliability.

Security in 5G networks is another area where QUIC contributes significant value. While 5G introduces network slicing and other advanced isolation mechanisms, individual IoT devices and applications must still protect their data flows against eavesdropping, tampering, and spoofing. QUIC's default use of modern cryptographic primitives and its encryption of transport headers bolster the end-to-end security posture of devices operating within 5G networks. Additionally, QUIC's built-in resistance to replay attacks and downgrade attempts enhances the protection of IoT systems in high-stakes environments, such as critical infrastructure or healthcare applications.

Beyond technical features, QUIC's user-space implementation makes it highly appealing for developers building IoT solutions on diverse hardware platforms. Many IoT devices rely on lightweight operating systems or embedded systems where integrating kernel-level protocols like TCP can be challenging. By contrast, QUIC libraries can be adapted to run in user space, offering developers greater control over transport-layer behaviors and facilitating rapid deployment of updates and improvements.

As IoT ecosystems expand into smart factories, connected healthcare, environmental monitoring, and consumer devices, the need for transport protocols that balance efficiency, security, and resilience becomes more pressing. QUIC is already being explored as a transport foundation for emerging IoT protocols and frameworks that demand reliable real-time communication and secure interoperability across heterogeneous networks. In 5G networks, where the promise of massive machine-type communications (mMTC) envisions billions of devices interacting concurrently, QUIC's efficiency in handling high-connection churn and its scalable design make it well-suited for such demanding use cases.

Ultimately, the intersection of QUIC with IoT and 5G highlights a broader trend of rethinking transport protocols for a hyper-connected, low-latency world. By reducing handshake overhead, enabling seamless mobility, and delivering encrypted-by-default communication, QUIC provides the critical infrastructure necessary to meet the unique challenges of IoT deployments operating on next-generation wireless networks. As both IoT and 5G ecosystems continue to evolve, QUIC is poised to become a foundational transport layer enabling secure, fast, and adaptive connectivity at unprecedented scales.

Satellite and High-Latency Networks

Satellite and high-latency networks present unique challenges for transport protocols due to their inherent long round-trip times, frequent packet loss, and variable link quality. Traditional transport protocols like TCP were not designed with such conditions in mind, often resulting in suboptimal performance. The use of QUIC in these environments introduces a set of features that address many of these challenges, positioning it as a strong candidate for improving connectivity in scenarios where users rely on satellite or other delay-prone infrastructures. As satellite internet providers expand their coverage and as high-latency networks remain critical for remote and underserved areas, QUIC is becoming an increasingly important component in delivering a more responsive and reliable user experience.

One of the primary difficulties in satellite networks is their high propagation delay. Geostationary satellites, for instance, are located approximately 35,786 kilometers above the Earth's surface, resulting in round-trip times (RTTs) that can exceed 500 milliseconds, even under ideal conditions. TCP's multi-step handshake process, which requires at least one full RTT to establish a connection and another for TLS negotiation, exacerbates latency in these environments. By contrast, QUIC reduces this initial delay by combining transport and encryption handshakes into a single round trip. When session resumption is available, QUIC can even transmit encrypted data immediately, eliminating the need for additional handshakes and allowing applications to deliver content faster despite the long distances involved.

Another key benefit of QUIC in satellite networks is its ability to mitigate head-of-line blocking at the transport layer. TCP enforces strict in-order delivery of packets, which means that the loss of a single packet delays all subsequent packets, even if those later packets have already arrived at the receiver. In satellite networks, where packet loss can be relatively frequent due to link instability or signal degradation, this behavior introduces significant delays. QUIC, by supporting multiplexed streams, avoids this bottleneck. Independent streams within a single QUIC connection can continue progressing even if one stream encounters packet loss. For applications such as web browsing or video streaming, this translates to faster resource loading and smoother playback, even under adverse network conditions.

QUIC's integrated loss detection and recovery mechanisms are also well-suited to the characteristics of high-latency environments. In TCP, loss recovery is often delayed due to reliance on duplicate acknowledgments and retransmission timeouts, both of which are exacerbated by long RTTs. QUIC's use of per-packet acknowledgments with explicit acknowledgment ranges allows for faster loss detection. Moreover, QUIC supports frame-level retransmissions rather than full-packet retransmissions, reducing redundancy and optimizing bandwidth usage—an important consideration in satellite networks, where bandwidth is often limited and expensive.

Congestion control in satellite and high-latency networks must also be adapted to the unique link characteristics. Traditional TCP congestion control algorithms, like Reno or Cubic, tend to interpret packet loss as a sign of congestion and respond by drastically reducing the sending rate. In satellite environments, however, packet loss is frequently caused by link-layer issues rather than network congestion. QUIC's modular congestion control design allows operators to deploy algorithms like BBR, which estimates available bandwidth and minimizes queuing delays without overreacting to non-congestion-related packet loss. This results in more stable throughput and lower latency, helping maintain acceptable performance for users connected via satellite.

The deployment of low Earth orbit (LEO) satellite constellations, such as those operated by SpaceX's Starlink and other emerging providers, further underscores the relevance of QUIC in modern satellite internet. LEO satellites orbit at much lower altitudes compared to geostationary satellites, resulting in reduced RTTs but introducing frequent handoffs as users transition between satellites. These handoffs can lead to IP address changes and routing shifts, disrupting traditional TCP connections. QUIC's connection migration feature is particularly beneficial in this context. By using connection identifiers that are decoupled from IP addresses, QUIC enables sessions to persist seamlessly as devices transition between satellite beams or hand off to ground stations, minimizing service interruptions and maintaining session continuity.

Security is another significant consideration in satellite and high-latency environments, where communications often traverse untrusted links and public network segments. QUIC's mandatory use of TLS 1.3 encryption ensures that both the data payload and most transport metadata are protected against eavesdropping and tampering. This is critical for users in remote areas where satellite links may be routed through third-party infrastructure or where governments may monitor or intercept traffic. By encrypting stream identifiers, packet numbers, and other transport headers, QUIC prevents adversaries from performing detailed traffic analysis, thereby enhancing user privacy and security.

From an operational perspective, the deployment of QUIC in satellite networks can reduce infrastructure complexity and cost. Because QUIC implements its transport logic in user space, providers can roll out updates and optimizations more rapidly than would be possible with kernel-level protocols like TCP. Additionally, QUIC's ability to consolidate multiple streams into a single connection reduces connection management overhead, a valuable feature in environments where network resources must be carefully optimized.

For users accessing cloud services, streaming platforms, or enterprise applications over satellite links, QUIC can lead to perceptible improvements in quality of experience. Web pages load faster, video buffering is reduced, and interactive applications such as video conferencing or online collaboration tools become more responsive. These improvements are critical in bridging the digital divide for populations in rural or remote regions where satellite remains one of the only viable options for broadband access.

Moreover, QUIC's extensibility opens the door to future optimizations tailored to satellite and high-latency networks. Features such as forward error correction (FEC), multipath QUIC (MP-QUIC), and network coding extensions are being actively explored by the research community to further enhance resilience and throughput in challenging environments. These innovations could enable QUIC to better handle packet loss bursts, fluctuating link quality, and dynamic routing scenarios that are common in satellite communications.

In maritime, aviation, and emergency response applications, where satellite networks provide critical connectivity for ships, aircraft, and disaster relief teams, QUIC's performance and resilience are particularly valuable. Real-time data feeds, voice communications, and telemetry exchanges benefit from QUIC's reduced latency and improved reliability, supporting mission-critical operations even in the most isolated or demanding environments.

The future of transport protocols in satellite and high-latency networks will continue to be shaped by QUIC's growing influence and the industry's shift toward encrypted, multiplexed, and adaptive communication layers. As satellite constellations expand coverage and technologies evolve to bring connectivity to the farthest reaches of the globe, QUIC will remain a key enabler of faster, more secure, and more reliable data transport for users navigating the unique challenges of space-based and long-distance terrestrial networks.

QUIC for Enterprise Networks

The adoption of QUIC in enterprise networks represents a significant shift in how organizations approach secure, high-performance transport protocols. Historically, enterprise environments have relied heavily on TCP for internal communications, remote access, and application delivery. However, as business applications evolve to demand lower latency, better security, and improved resilience to network changes, QUIC emerges as a modern transport protocol capable of meeting these new challenges. Its ability to streamline connection establishment, eliminate head-of-line blocking, and provide built-in encryption positions it as a powerful tool for enterprises looking to modernize their networking stacks and optimize both internal and external communications.

One of the most compelling advantages of QUIC for enterprise networks is its ability to reduce connection setup latency. In environments where employees frequently access cloud-hosted applications, virtual desktops, or remote collaboration tools, every millisecond of delay adds up, impacting productivity and user satisfaction. Traditional TCP-based connections, particularly when combined with TLS 1.2, require multiple round trips before data can flow securely. QUIC addresses this inefficiency by combining the transport and security handshakes into a single round trip through its integration with TLS 1.3. For internal enterprise applications or cloud services accessed over VPNs or SD-WANs, this translates into faster session establishment and improved responsiveness for critical business workflows.

Security is a major concern in any enterprise network, and QUIC's security model provides a robust framework to address modern threats. Unlike TCP, which leaves transport headers exposed to the network, QUIC encrypts nearly all transport metadata, including packet numbers, stream identifiers, and acknowledgment frames. This reduces the visibility of internal application behavior to potential attackers and mitigates common exploits such as session hijacking, injection attacks, or replay attacks. QUIC's encryption of both application and transport layers ensures that sensitive data transmitted between enterprise endpoints, whether employees working remotely or systems within data centers, remains protected from interception and tampering.

In addition to improving security, QUIC's stream multiplexing has significant implications for enterprise application performance. Many modern business applications, particularly web-based platforms and SaaS tools, require the simultaneous transmission of multiple data streams. Under TCP, these streams are multiplexed at the application layer but share the same transport connection, making them susceptible to head-of-line blocking. QUIC eliminates this bottleneck by natively supporting multiple independent streams within a single connection. For enterprise applications like customer relationship management (CRM) platforms, enterprise resource planning (ERP) systems, or intranet portals, this leads to faster loading times and smoother user experiences, especially in networks with variable latency or packet loss.

Enterprise networks are also characterized by their diversity of endpoints and the need to support mobility. With the rise of hybrid work models, employees frequently switch between corporate Wi-Fi, home networks, and mobile connections throughout their workday. TCP-based connections often break when such transitions occur due to changes in IP addresses or routing paths, forcing users to reconnect to corporate services. QUIC addresses this challenge through its connection migration feature. By decoupling session identifiers from IP addresses via opaque connection IDs, QUIC allows enterprise applications to maintain session continuity even as users roam between different networks or transition from Wi-Fi to 5G. This seamless mobility enhances productivity and reduces frustration for remote and mobile workers.

In distributed enterprise environments, where organizations maintain multiple branch offices, data centers, and cloud regions, QUIC also supports more efficient inter-service communication. Microservices deployed across different regions or hybrid cloud environments can leverage QUIC's multiplexing and connection migration capabilities to improve resilience and reduce latency in service-to-service interactions. Enterprise service meshes, which facilitate secure communication between microservices, can integrate QUIC as a transport layer to benefit from its encryption, stream isolation, and customizable congestion control mechanisms. These advantages are especially relevant for business-critical applications that demand low latency and high availability, such as financial transaction systems or real-time data processing pipelines.

Enterprise networks frequently operate under strict compliance and regulatory requirements related to data protection and privacy. QUIC's strong encryption model helps organizations meet these obligations by ensuring that sensitive information, including internal application data and user credentials, is secured during transit. Moreover, QUIC's encryption of transport headers prevents third-party intermediaries, such as ISPs or external network operators, from gleaning insights into enterprise traffic patterns or application behaviors. This reduces the risk of inadvertent data leakage and supports adherence to data privacy frameworks such as GDPR, HIPAA, and PCI DSS.

The deployment of QUIC in enterprise networks also intersects with modern network architectures like SD-WAN and Zero Trust Network Access (ZTNA). In SD-WAN environments, where enterprises seek to optimize and secure traffic across multiple WAN links, QUIC's efficiency in handling variable latency and packet loss improves overall application performance. SD-WAN controllers can leverage QUIC's encrypted transport and congestion control features to better manage traffic between branch offices and cloud applications. In Zero Trust environments, where every connection is treated as potentially untrusted, QUIC's mandatory encryption, coupled with its ability to reduce the attack surface at the transport layer, aligns well with Zero Trust principles.

Observability and troubleshooting are essential considerations for enterprise network operations teams, and QUIC's design introduces new dynamics in this area. Since QUIC encrypts most transport-level metadata, traditional monitoring tools that rely on deep packet inspection may be less effective. To address this, enterprise IT teams are increasingly adopting endpoint-based observability frameworks that collect metrics directly from client and server systems. Standards such as qlog allow enterprises to gather insights into QUIC session behavior, including stream activity, congestion window adjustments, and packet loss events, while respecting the protocol's privacy-preserving design. These insights help IT teams diagnose network issues, optimize performance, and ensure the smooth operation of business-critical applications.

Enterprise adoption of QUIC also has implications for cost optimization. By improving application responsiveness and reducing latency-related inefficiencies, QUIC contributes to better user productivity and reduced infrastructure overhead. For example, QUIC's efficient use of bandwidth and ability to minimize retransmissions result in lower data transfer costs, particularly in cloud-hosted applications that operate under metered pricing models. Additionally, by supporting faster session establishment and streamlining transport-level operations, QUIC can reduce server resource consumption, enabling enterprises to scale applications more effectively and reduce operating expenses.

As enterprise IT strategies continue to shift toward cloud-native architectures, mobile-first access models, and highly distributed workforces, the demand for modern, flexible transport protocols will only grow. QUIC offers enterprises a forward-looking solution that addresses both current pain points and emerging requirements. Its ability to deliver secure, low-latency, and resilient connectivity across varied network conditions positions it as a foundational technology for enterprise networks seeking to modernize their digital infrastructure. Whether deployed for external-facing applications, internal services, or hybrid cloud architectures, QUIC stands to play a pivotal role in helping organizations meet the performance, security, and reliability expectations of the modern enterprise environment.

Regulatory and Compliance Aspects

The deployment of QUIC in enterprise and consumer networks raises a variety of regulatory and compliance considerations that organizations must address. As QUIC continues to gain adoption across sectors ranging from financial services to healthcare and government, ensuring that its technical capabilities align with regulatory requirements is critical. Transport protocols, though often perceived as technical details, play a direct role in shaping how organizations protect user data, manage risk, and demonstrate adherence to legal frameworks. QUIC's strong encryption, reduced metadata exposure, and user-space implementation model present both opportunities and challenges in meeting the compliance needs of highly regulated industries.

One of the most significant aspects of QUIC relevant to regulatory frameworks is its mandatory use of TLS 1.3 encryption. Many modern regulations, including the European Union's General Data Protection Regulation (GDPR), the Health Insurance Portability and Accountability Act (HIPAA) in the United States, and the Payment Card Industry Data Security Standard (PCI DSS), require organizations to protect sensitive data in transit. QUIC fulfills this requirement by encrypting not only application-layer payloads but also most transport-layer metadata. The encryption of stream identifiers, packet numbers, and acknowledgment frames enhances data confidentiality and integrity during transmission, reducing the risk of data interception or manipulation by unauthorized third parties.

However, the same privacy-enhancing features that improve security also complicate compliance with certain regulatory mandates related to monitoring and auditing. Some financial regulations, for example, require enterprises to log and archive transactional data or to provide detailed network activity records for audit purposes. With QUIC encrypting much of the transport-layer metadata, traditional network-based monitoring tools that rely on inspecting TCP headers or unencrypted packet flows lose visibility into connection behaviors. Enterprises deploying QUIC in regulated environments must therefore implement endpoint-based logging mechanisms to capture necessary details such as session start and end times, data transfer volumes, and connection performance metrics. Standards like qlog provide a foundation for generating structured logs that can support audit and compliance workflows without compromising QUIC's security model.

Data sovereignty requirements, which mandate that sensitive data must remain within specific geographic boundaries, also intersect with QUIC's deployment. Organizations subject to data localization laws must ensure that QUIC sessions, especially in cloud-hosted applications or globally distributed services, do not inadvertently transfer personal or regulated data across borders. Although QUIC encrypts data during transit, enterprises are still responsible for ensuring that traffic routing, server selection, and data residency policies adhere to jurisdictional mandates. This may involve configuring QUIC-compatible content delivery networks (CDNs) and cloud services to limit endpoint availability based on regional or national regulations.

A further consideration is lawful intercept, where telecommunications providers or service operators may be subject to government-mandated interception orders requiring them to provide access to certain communications. With QUIC's pervasive encryption and its resistance to passive surveillance, fulfilling lawful intercept requests becomes more complex compared to legacy protocols like TCP, where metadata is more readily accessible. While QUIC does not preclude compliance with lawful intercept laws, it shifts the focus from network-level interception to endpoint cooperation, placing greater responsibility on service providers to implement lawful intercept capabilities at the application or service layer.

Compliance with industry-specific regulations, such as those enforced in healthcare, finance, or critical infrastructure sectors, also intersects with QUIC's deployment. For example, healthcare providers operating under HIPAA must ensure that electronic protected health information (ePHI) is transmitted securely and that access to such data is auditable. While QUIC's encryption helps satisfy the requirement for data security, healthcare organizations must supplement this with robust logging, access control, and incident response mechanisms to demonstrate compliance. In financial services, regulations like the Gramm-Leach-Bliley Act (GLBA) and standards enforced by financial regulators may similarly require demonstrable safeguards for customer data and transaction integrity, which QUIC's encryption model supports but does not fully address on its own.

An emerging concern is the interplay between QUIC and network neutrality or traffic management regulations. Because QUIC encrypts much of its metadata, it can limit the ability of network operators to apply traffic-shaping or prioritization policies based on flow characteristics. This raises questions for regulators about how network operators can maintain transparency and fairness while respecting user privacy. Some regulatory frameworks require operators to disclose their traffic management practices, and QUIC's encryption could complicate compliance if operators are unable to distinguish between different traffic types for legitimate purposes, such as ensuring the performance of emergency services.

Additionally, privacy regulations such as the California Consumer Privacy Act (CCPA) and GDPR include provisions around minimizing data collection and protecting user anonymity. By encrypting transport headers and reducing the exposure of identifying information, QUIC aligns well with privacy-by-design principles emphasized in these laws. However, organizations must still carefully assess how their QUIC implementations handle identifiers like IP addresses, connection IDs, and application-layer data to avoid inadvertently violating privacy mandates. For instance, while QUIC itself limits metadata exposure, an application running on top of QUIC could still leak identifying information through HTTP headers or other unencrypted content.

Regulators are also beginning to pay closer attention to how next-generation transport protocols like QUIC impact forensic investigations and incident response activities. In environments where encrypted transport obscures traditional forensic signals, incident responders may need to rely on endpoint logs, telemetry data, and behavioral analytics to investigate security incidents or compliance breaches. This creates a need for organizations to strengthen endpoint-level monitoring capabilities and to maintain detailed records of application-level activity that can supplement encrypted transport-layer traffic with actionable insights.

Finally, international regulatory bodies and standards organizations are increasingly acknowledging the role that QUIC and similar protocols will play in the evolving internet landscape. Discussions are underway in groups such as the IETF and regional regulatory authorities to balance the benefits of encrypted transport with the operational and legal needs of enterprises and governments. These discussions may shape future guidance or technical recommendations on deploying QUIC in compliance-sensitive environments, potentially influencing best practices for key management, telemetry collection, and incident response.

For organizations operating in regulated industries, the adoption of QUIC presents both an opportunity to modernize transport security and a challenge to adapt existing compliance processes. While QUIC strengthens data protection and aligns with global trends toward encryption and privacy, enterprises must proactively implement complementary controls to meet regulatory expectations. This includes enhancing endpoint observability, maintaining clear records of data flows, and collaborating with legal, security, and compliance teams to develop policies that fully leverage QUIC's capabilities while addressing compliance requirements.

As regulators, standards bodies, and industry stakeholders continue to assess the impact of QUIC on compliance and oversight, organizations must stay informed and agile, ensuring that their transport-layer innovations support both their technical goals and their legal obligations in an increasingly regulated digital landscape.

Open-Source Implementations

The open-source community has played a vital role in the evolution and adoption of QUIC, offering a diverse range of implementations that have accelerated the protocol's maturity and helped foster widespread industry acceptance. By making QUIC accessible to developers, researchers, and enterprises worldwide, these projects have contributed significantly to both standardization efforts and practical deployments. Open-source QUIC stacks serve as the foundation for production systems, testing environments, and educational initiatives, offering insight into the protocol's inner workings and enabling rapid iteration and innovation.

Among the most prominent open-source implementations is quic-go, an implementation written in the Go programming language. quic-go has gained substantial traction due to Go's popularity among developers building cloud-native and distributed applications. The library supports both QUIC transport and HTTP/3, making it suitable for building web servers, reverse proxies, and other backend services. quic-go is actively maintained, with contributions from both independent developers and organizations like Google and Cloudflare, ensuring that it remains up to date with the latest developments in the QUIC and HTTP/3 standards. One of the strengths of quic-go is its modular design, which allows developers to experiment with different congestion control algorithms, TLS configurations, and stream management strategies in a flexible, user-friendly environment.

Another widely used implementation is ngtcp2, written in C, which has become a popular choice for low-level systems development and embedded systems. ngtcp2 is designed to offer a minimal yet highly efficient QUIC transport library, focusing on performance and compliance with the IETF QUIC specifications. It is often used in combination with nghttp3, a companion library that implements HTTP/3 on top of ngtcp2. The ngtcp2 project has been instrumental in providing developers with a lightweight alternative suitable for integrating QUIC into applications where resource constraints are a concern, such as IoT devices or performance-critical services. The project's focus on adhering closely to the QUIC RFCs makes it a valuable reference implementation for developers aiming to ensure interoperability and protocol correctness.

msquic, Microsoft's open-source QUIC implementation, has emerged as a critical component of the Windows networking stack and Microsoft Azure services. Written in C and designed with a strong emphasis on performance, msquic supports both user-space and kernel-mode operation, allowing it to be integrated into a variety of system architectures. Microsoft has deployed msquic extensively in production environments, powering QUIC-based communication in products like Microsoft Teams and Azure's service mesh. By open-sourcing msquic under the MIT license, Microsoft has contributed a high-performance, enterprise-grade QUIC implementation that benefits the wider developer community and fosters cross-platform interoperability.

Cloudflare has contributed to the open-source QUIC ecosystem with quiche, a Rust-based QUIC implementation that emphasizes security, performance, and safe memory handling. Rust's memory safety guarantees align well with the security goals of transport protocol development, making quiche a popular choice for projects where safety and robustness are paramount. quiche has been adopted internally at Cloudflare to power HTTP/3 services at the edge, providing QUIC-based acceleration for millions of websites. The project also includes support for common use cases such as server and client implementations, load balancing, and integration with TLS libraries like rustls. quiche's focus on extensibility makes it attractive to developers experimenting with advanced features like multipath QUIC (MP-QUIC) or custom frame types.

Picoquic is another lightweight implementation, written in C and designed specifically for embedded systems and environments with constrained resources. Picoquic is notable for its compact codebase and efficient memory usage, making it well-suited for use in IoT devices, network appliances, and experimental platforms. Despite its small footprint, picoquic supports a full range of QUIC features, including connection migration, stream multiplexing, and TLS 1.3 encryption. The project's emphasis on simplicity and portability has attracted interest from developers working on edge computing applications and research initiatives that require a customizable and easily deployable QUIC stack.

The diversity of open-source QUIC implementations highlights the protocol's adaptability across different programming languages, system architectures, and deployment environments. Developers can select implementations that align with their technical goals, whether optimizing for speed, security, resource efficiency, or ease of integration with existing codebases. This variety also promotes healthy competition and collaboration, as contributors from different projects regularly participate in interoperability testing events and working group discussions to ensure that implementations conform to the evolving standards set by the IETF.

Open-source QUIC libraries have also played a crucial role in interoperability testing, a key factor in the protocol's successful standardization. During IETF hackathons and formal interop events, teams representing different implementations—including quic-go, ngtcp2, msquic, quiche, and picoquic—routinely validate that their stacks work seamlessly with one another under a variety of network conditions and protocol configurations. These collaborative efforts have uncovered ambiguities in draft specifications, exposed subtle implementation bugs, and informed best practices that continue to improve the reliability and performance of QUIC deployments worldwide.

In addition to powering production systems, open-source QUIC stacks serve as valuable tools for education and research. Universities, research labs, and independent developers leverage these implementations to study transport-layer behavior, evaluate novel congestion control algorithms, and prototype enhancements to the core protocol. The availability of open-source code facilitates a deeper understanding of QUIC's internal mechanics, providing a resource for students and engineers who wish to explore advanced networking concepts in a hands-on, practical context.

Open-source contributions have also been instrumental in extending QUIC beyond its initial HTTP/3 focus. Experimental projects are using QUIC as a foundation for new transport-layer protocols, such as DNS-over-QUIC (DoQ), and for custom applications requiring secure, low-latency data delivery. The flexibility and accessibility of open-source QUIC stacks enable developers to rapidly iterate and deploy innovative solutions in domains ranging from edge computing and 5G networks to real-time media delivery and peer-to-peer communication.

As QUIC adoption continues to grow, the open-source ecosystem will remain a cornerstone of its success. These implementations not only help drive protocol evolution and best practices but also democratize access to cutting-edge transport technology, empowering organizations of all sizes to integrate QUIC into their services. The collaborative spirit of the open-source community ensures that QUIC will continue to evolve in response to emerging technical challenges, securing its role as a foundational component of the modern internet.

Major Tech Giants and QUIC Adoption

The adoption of QUIC by major technology companies has been one of the driving forces behind the protocol's rapid rise to prominence in the global internet ecosystem. From the initial experimental deployment by Google to widespread support from Microsoft, Meta, Cloudflare, and other leading tech firms, QUIC has evolved from a promising innovation to a production-grade transport protocol shaping the way users experience modern digital services. These early and large-scale adopters not only validated QUIC's technical merits but also catalyzed its adoption across a wide range of industries and applications.

Google was the first and most significant player to champion QUIC, having introduced the protocol within its ecosystem as early as 2013. Initially implemented to improve the performance of its own services, Google deployed QUIC to accelerate the delivery of content on products like Google Search, Gmail, YouTube, and Google Drive. Given Google's global infrastructure and its focus on improving web performance for users on mobile and high-latency networks, QUIC was a natural fit. Google's deployment led to significant performance improvements, particularly for YouTube users, who experienced reduced video startup times and fewer rebuffering events, especially on unreliable mobile networks. Google's ability to conduct real-world testing at massive scale provided valuable insights into loss recovery, congestion control, and stream multiplexing, many of which informed the later standardization process at the IETF.

Following Google's lead, Meta (formerly Facebook) began integrating QUIC across its suite of services, including Facebook, Instagram, and WhatsApp. Meta's infrastructure team recognized the protocol's ability to deliver faster and more reliable connections to its predominantly mobile user base, which often operates under suboptimal network conditions. By leveraging QUIC's stream multiplexing and reduced connection establishment latency, Meta was able to improve content delivery times and reduce the frequency of connection drops, particularly for users in developing regions with limited bandwidth or high network variability. For applications like Instagram, where rapid loading of multimedia content is central to the user experience, QUIC contributed to smoother scrolling and faster rendering of images and videos.

Cloudflare, one of the world's leading content delivery networks (CDNs) and security providers, was an early advocate for the IETF version of QUIC and HTTP/3. Cloudflare's role in the internet infrastructure space enabled it to bring QUIC's benefits to millions of websites served through its edge network. By offering QUIC and HTTP/3 support by default on its CDN, Cloudflare helped popularize the protocol beyond the walled gardens of individual tech giants and into the broader web ecosystem. Websites and applications using

Cloudflare saw improvements in page load times, especially in regions where high-latency networks previously hindered performance. Cloudflare also highlighted the security benefits of QUIC, promoting it as a means to reduce the attack surface at the transport layer through encryption of nearly all transport headers.

Microsoft's adoption of QUIC further cemented its position as a transport protocol for modern applications. Microsoft's implementation, msquic, became the core transport layer for key products such as Microsoft Teams and Azure's service mesh infrastructure. In collaboration-heavy applications like Teams, where video calls, file sharing, and chat interactions occur concurrently, QUIC's ability to multiplex independent streams ensured that performance remained consistent even in congested network environments. Microsoft's use of QUIC in Azure's service mesh also enabled microservices deployed across Azure regions to communicate securely and efficiently, reducing service-to-service latency and improving the scalability of distributed applications.

Amazon Web Services (AWS) has also moved toward supporting QUIC and HTTP/3 within its CloudFront CDN and Elastic Load Balancing (ELB) services. This has allowed AWS customers to improve the performance of web and API traffic distributed via AWS's global infrastructure. The inclusion of QUIC within AWS's product offerings reflects the growing demand from enterprise customers to leverage the protocol's advantages for customer-facing applications and internal workloads alike.

Mozilla, the organization behind the Firefox browser, played a key role in promoting QUIC's adoption among end users. Firefox's support for QUIC and HTTP/3 ensures that millions of users benefit from faster and more secure browsing experiences on websites that have enabled the protocol. Mozilla's commitment to open standards and privacy aligned well with QUIC's focus on encrypting transport metadata, reducing the ability of network intermediaries to perform traffic analysis on user sessions.

In the streaming space, companies like Netflix and YouTube have incorporated QUIC into their delivery pipelines to optimize the viewer experience. Streaming platforms operate under strict latency and performance requirements, where connection stability and throughput variability can directly impact video quality and playback smoothness. QUIC's fast connection establishment and adaptive congestion control help these services deliver higher quality streams with fewer interruptions, even under adverse network conditions. Netflix, in particular, has experimented with using QUIC to improve the performance of its streaming protocol stack, further advancing its efforts to provide ultra-low-latency video delivery to a global audience.

Beyond the major technology firms, telecommunications providers and mobile network operators are increasingly embracing QUIC to improve customer experience across their services. Operators such as Vodafone and Orange have explored how QUIC can optimize network utilization while enhancing user-perceived performance for mobile applications. QUIC's ability to recover quickly from packet loss and to maintain session persistence across network transitions aligns well with the challenges faced by mobile operators managing traffic on 4G and 5G networks.

The collective impact of these tech giants adopting QUIC has not only accelerated its deployment but also contributed to its refinement. Lessons learned from large-scale implementations have been fed back into the open-source community and standards bodies, influencing best practices around congestion control algorithms, observability tools, and operational guidance for QUIC deployments. The momentum generated by major technology companies has also prompted cloud providers, CDN operators, and independent developers to integrate QUIC into their products and services, resulting in a wider ecosystem of support that spans web browsers, mobile applications, backend APIs, and microservice architectures.

The adoption of QUIC by these industry leaders serves as a clear signal of its transformative potential. As QUIC continues to replace TCP in an increasing number of applications and services, its role as the transport layer for the modern internet becomes more firmly established. The leadership of these tech giants in adopting, deploying, and advocating for QUIC has paved the way for broader industry acceptance and has helped establish QUIC as a cornerstone of next-generation digital infrastructure.

QUIC Performance Tuning

Tuning QUIC for optimal performance is both an art and a science, requiring a deep understanding of the protocol's architecture, network conditions, and application-specific requirements. While QUIC offers numerous advantages over traditional transport protocols, such as reduced handshake latency, multiplexing without head-of-line blocking, and built-in encryption, achieving the highest possible performance in production environments demands careful configuration and continuous monitoring. QUIC's user-space implementation model offers a high degree of flexibility, allowing developers and network engineers to fine-tune various parameters to suit diverse use cases ranging from web applications to real-time media and enterprise services.

One of the most fundamental areas for performance tuning in QUIC is congestion control. QUIC is designed to be congestion control agnostic, meaning implementers can choose from a variety of algorithms based on their specific goals. While the QUIC specification recommends a baseline congestion control scheme modeled after TCP's Reno and Cubic algorithms, many production deployments have adopted BBR (Bottleneck Bandwidth and Round-trip propagation time) due to its ability to deliver high throughput and minimize latency. BBR estimates bottleneck bandwidth and RTT independently of packet loss, making it especially effective in networks where loss may not correlate with congestion, such as wireless and satellite links. Tuning congestion control involves adjusting parameters like initial congestion window size, pacing rates, and gain factors to balance throughput, latency, and fairness depending on the application's traffic patterns.

Another critical factor in tuning QUIC is the optimization of handshake behavior. QUIC supports 0-RTT resumption, allowing clients to send encrypted application data immediately after completing a previous session. However, enabling 0-RTT requires careful management of session resumption tickets and consideration of replay risks. Applications that can tolerate the trade-offs of 0-RTT, such as idempotent GET requests in web browsing or media streaming scenarios, stand to benefit from faster time-to-first-byte metrics. For applications where stateful operations or sensitive transactions occur early in a session, disabling or restricting o-RTT may be more appropriate to mitigate security risks.

Tuning flow control windows at both the connection and stream levels is another area that can have a significant impact on performance. QUIC's flow control mechanisms limit the amount of data a sender can transmit before receiving acknowledgment from the receiver, preventing resource exhaustion and promoting fairness. However, conservative default flow control settings can result in underutilization of available bandwidth, particularly in high-capacity networks. By increasing the initial maximum data limits and stream-level credit values, operators can reduce the likelihood of sender stalls and improve overall throughput. It is essential to strike a balance, as overly aggressive flow control settings may lead to excessive memory consumption on the receiver, particularly in resource-constrained environments.

Packet pacing is another lever that can be adjusted to optimize QUIC's performance. Pacing helps distribute packet bursts more evenly over time, smoothing traffic and reducing the likelihood of congestion-related packet loss. Implementers can tune pacing rates based on real-time network measurements, RTT estimates, and congestion window growth to achieve better bandwidth utilization without overwhelming intermediary devices such as routers and switches. Fine-tuning pacing is especially critical in data center environments and mobile networks, where sudden traffic bursts can result in queue buildup and increased latency.

Tuning the maximum packet size, or Maximum Transmission Unit (MTU), is also important for maximizing QUIC's efficiency. QUIC packets are encapsulated in UDP datagrams, and selecting an optimal MTU helps ensure that packets are transmitted without fragmentation at the IP layer. In most internet scenarios, an MTU of 1350 to 1400 bytes is recommended to account for typical UDP and IP header overhead while avoiding fragmentation on path MTUs around 1500 bytes. However, in controlled environments like data centers or private networks where jumbo frames are supported, it may be possible to safely increase the MTU for better payload efficiency and reduced per-packet overhead.

Observability plays a crucial role in performance tuning, as adjustments must be guided by empirical data gathered from real-world traffic. Implementers should leverage structured logging, metrics collection, and tracing tools such as qlog and qvis to capture insights into connection behavior, packet loss events, RTT fluctuations, and congestion window dynamics. Monitoring metrics such as packet retransmission rates, handshake durations, stream-level throughput, and congestion control state transitions helps identify bottlenecks and fine-tune parameters for specific workloads and environments.

For applications that prioritize user experience, such as video streaming platforms or interactive web applications, stream prioritization tuning can yield significant benefits. QUIC allows applications to define priorities for individual streams, ensuring that critical resources—such as HTML, CSS, or initial video segments—are delivered ahead of less urgent assets like background images or analytics beacons. Implementers can configure custom prioritization schemes tailored to their applications' loading patterns, improving perceived responsiveness and reducing page load times.

In scenarios where QUIC is deployed over high-latency or unreliable networks, additional tuning may involve experimenting with experimental extensions such as Forward Error Correction (FEC) or loss-resilient frame types. While FEC introduces additional overhead, it can help reduce the impact of burst losses by proactively including redundant data in transmissions. Implementers must weigh the trade-offs between increased bandwidth usage and improved reliability based on the characteristics of their target networks.

Security-related tuning also influences performance. Selecting optimized cryptographic libraries, such as those offering hardware-accelerated AES-GCM or ChaCha20-Poly1305, can reduce the CPU cost associated with encrypting and decrypting QUIC packets. Ensuring that TLS session ticket lifetimes and rotation policies are configured appropriately helps minimize the operational costs of resumption without introducing risks related to key reuse or session replay.

Finally, tuning QUIC's connection ID rotation policies is important for maintaining both performance and privacy. While frequent rotation of connection IDs helps mitigate linkability and tracking concerns, excessively short rotation intervals can introduce operational overhead by requiring frequent revalidation of connection state and increased token exchange traffic. Finding a balance between security and operational efficiency ensures that session privacy is preserved without degrading transport performance.

Ultimately, QUIC performance tuning is a continuous process that requires holistic consideration of the application's requirements, user demographics, and network environments. The flexibility of QUIC's design allows for extensive optimization opportunities, empowering operators and developers to deliver high-performance, secure, and reliable services to users around the globe. By combining real-time telemetry, intelligent default settings, and iterative experimentation, organizations can fully unlock QUIC's potential as a transport protocol built for modern internet applications.

The Evolution of Congestion Algorithms

The history of internet congestion control is deeply intertwined with the evolution of transport protocols and the growing complexity of global networks. From the early days of TCP's primitive congestion avoidance mechanisms to modern algorithms designed for high-throughput and low-latency applications, the evolution of congestion algorithms has been marked by a continuous balancing act between fairness, efficiency, and adaptability. Congestion control plays a critical role in maintaining the stability of the internet by ensuring that multiple users can share network resources without degrading overall performance. As QUIC emerged as a modern transport protocol, it inherited the lessons learned from decades of TCP congestion control research while introducing flexibility to experiment with new approaches.

The earliest congestion control algorithms, developed in the 1980s, were reactive and rudimentary. TCP's initial implementation lacked any real mechanism to handle congestion, leading to the now-infamous congestion collapse events where network links became saturated with retransmitted packets, effectively grinding communication to a halt. The seminal work of Van Jacobson introduced concepts like slow start, congestion avoidance, and fast retransmit, forming the basis of the first practical congestion control strategy. The slow start algorithm, in particular, was designed to probe available bandwidth cautiously by starting with a small congestion window and exponentially increasing it until packet loss signaled the onset of congestion.

Over time, additional refinements were made to TCP's congestion control, resulting in algorithms such as Reno, Tahoe, and NewReno. These algorithms introduced techniques like fast recovery, which helped avoid returning to slow start unnecessarily after detecting packet loss via triple duplicate acknowledgments. While effective on traditional wired networks with relatively stable conditions, these algorithms struggled in high-latency or wireless environments where non-congestion-related packet loss could mislead the congestion control logic and trigger unnecessary reductions in the sending rate.

As internet usage grew and bandwidth demands increased, the community recognized the need for more aggressive algorithms to make better use of available capacity. Cubic, introduced in the mid-2000s, became one of the most widely adopted TCP congestion control algorithms, particularly in Linux-based systems. Cubic departs from the linear window growth of Reno, instead using a cubic function to grow the congestion window more rapidly after packet loss, particularly in high-bandwidth and long-delay networks. Cubic's success lies in its ability to recover more quickly and fully utilize modern high-capacity links while still maintaining TCP-friendliness, meaning it behaves fairly when coexisting with legacy TCP flows.

With the rise of data centers, cloud computing, and real-time applications, congestion control research began shifting toward low-latency algorithms that prioritized responsiveness alongside throughput. Data center traffic patterns, characterized by short-lived flows and bursty workloads, created a demand for congestion control algorithms that could minimize queuing delays and deliver predictable performance under heavy load. This led to the development of Data Center TCP (DCTCP), which uses Explicit Congestion Notification

(ECN) marks to fine-tune window growth without waiting for packet drops. DCTCP's ability to react to early congestion signals reduced latency and queuing delays within data centers, making it ideal for latency-sensitive applications such as distributed storage systems and online transaction processing.

The emergence of BBR (Bottleneck Bandwidth and Round-trip propagation time) marked a paradigm shift in congestion control philosophy. Unlike traditional loss-based algorithms like Reno and Cubic, BBR seeks to model the network path by estimating available bottleneck bandwidth and RTT. This model-driven approach allows BBR to maintain high throughput and low latency even on lossy or variable-delay links, where loss alone is not a reliable congestion signal. BBR periodically probes for bandwidth increases while keeping queues shallow, making it highly effective in environments such as wireless networks or high-speed backbone links where legacy algorithms may oscillate between underutilization and bufferbloat. Since its deployment in Google services, BBR has gained popularity among cloud providers and content delivery networks seeking to optimize traffic performance across diverse internet paths.

The flexibility of QUIC has accelerated the exploration of congestion control beyond traditional TCP ecosystems. Unlike TCP, which relies on operating system kernels for congestion control behavior, QUIC implementations typically reside in user space. This shift allows developers to customize congestion algorithms at the application layer, enabling rapid experimentation and deployment of alternative strategies. Within the QUIC ecosystem, multiple algorithms coexist, including Cubic, BBR, and experimental approaches such as Hybrid Slow Start, which combines slow start with pacing techniques to avoid packet bursts.

Additionally, QUIC's extensibility supports ongoing research into multipath congestion control, where connections leverage multiple network interfaces simultaneously to enhance reliability and throughput. Algorithms tailored for multipath environments must balance traffic distribution across paths with varying capacities and latencies while preventing congestion on any single path. This new frontier in congestion control introduces additional complexity but offers substantial gains in performance for mobile devices, edge computing, and next-generation wireless networks.

The evolution of congestion algorithms is also being shaped by the growing emphasis on fairness and coexistence. In heterogeneous networks where flows may use different algorithms or transport protocols, ensuring that one flow does not monopolize resources at the expense of others remains a key challenge. Algorithms such as BBR have prompted research into fairness models, as their behavior can outperform loss-based algorithms in certain scenarios. This has led to ongoing efforts to fine-tune BBR and develop hybrid strategies that balance throughput maximization with equitable resource distribution among competing flows.

Machine learning and AI are emerging as promising tools to further evolve congestion control. Adaptive algorithms that leverage real-time telemetry and predictive models can dynamically adjust congestion window sizes, pacing rates, and probing intervals based on observed network conditions. While still largely experimental, AI-assisted congestion control could unlock significant improvements in environments characterized by highly variable latency, such as mobile networks and satellite links.

The evolution of congestion algorithms reflects a broader trend in networking: the need to accommodate increasingly diverse application requirements and network architectures. From traditional loss-based strategies to cutting-edge model-driven and hybrid approaches, congestion control has adapted to the shifting demands of cloud computing, real-time media, IoT, and mobile connectivity. As QUIC continues to proliferate across modern internet services, its ability to support flexible, modular congestion control will empower developers to push the boundaries of what is possible at the transport layer, ushering in a new era of highly optimized, application-aware network performance.

Case Study: QUIC at Google Scale

The deployment of QUIC at Google scale represents one of the most ambitious and impactful transport protocol rollouts in the history of the internet. As both the birthplace of QUIC and its earliest large-scale adopter, Google has demonstrated how a modern, flexible transport layer can transform user experience and operational efficiency across a vast, globally distributed infrastructure. With services like Google Search, Gmail, Google Drive, and YouTube serving billions of users, Google provided the ideal proving ground for QUIC's performance and resilience under real-world conditions.

The origins of QUIC at Google were rooted in the company's desire to reduce latency for end users, particularly in mobile and emerging markets where variable network conditions often degrade application responsiveness. Google's engineering teams recognized that TCP, despite decades of optimizations, struggled in environments with high packet loss, frequent network transitions, and elevated round-trip times. Additionally, the multiple round trips required by TCP combined with TLS handshakes contributed to noticeable delays during connection establishment. Google envisioned a transport protocol that could reduce these inefficiencies while also embedding encryption as a default security feature.

The initial experimental version of QUIC was deployed within Google's Chrome browser and its backend services in 2013. The decision to integrate QUIC into Chrome allowed Google to control both the client and server-side implementations, enabling fine-tuned optimizations and rapid feedback loops. Early A/B tests showed promising results, with a noticeable reduction in page load times and improved video streaming performance for users on congested or unreliable networks. This success led to the gradual expansion of QUIC across Google's services, eventually covering Search, YouTube, Ads, and Google Cloud products.

At the core of Google's QUIC deployment strategy was the use of its extensive edge infrastructure. Google's global network of data centers and edge points of presence enabled the company to minimize the physical distance between clients and servers, enhancing QUIC's latency benefits. QUIC's integration with Google's edge caches ensured that user requests were terminated as close to the user as possible, enabling faster handshakes and more efficient content delivery. The synergy between QUIC's design and Google's edge network proved especially effective in regions with less reliable connectivity, such as parts of Africa, Southeast Asia, and Latin America.

One of the most significant performance gains came from QUIC's ability to eliminate head-of-line blocking at the transport layer. Google observed that, under TCP, a single lost packet in a multiplexed HTTP/2 connection could delay the delivery of subsequent streams, impacting the perceived speed of services like YouTube. By contrast, QUIC's support for independent stream multiplexing ensured that critical assets such as video segments, metadata, and control frames could continue flowing even if packet loss occurred on other streams. The result was a smoother playback experience with fewer buffering interruptions, particularly for users with poor network conditions.

Google also leveraged QUIC's connection migration capabilities to address the needs of its mobile user base. Mobile users frequently switch between Wi-Fi and cellular networks or experience IP address changes due to NAT rebinding. TCP connections often broke under these conditions, forcing applications to re-establish sessions, which incurred additional latency. QUIC's use of connection identifiers decoupled session state from specific IP addresses, allowing connections to survive network transitions seamlessly. This led to measurable improvements in session continuity for applications like Google Maps and Google Drive, where users frequently move between networks while using the service.

At Google scale, observability and performance monitoring were critical components of the QUIC deployment. Google's infrastructure teams developed custom telemetry pipelines to gather detailed metrics on QUIC's behavior across billions of sessions. These metrics included handshake completion times, loss recovery rates, congestion window dynamics, and stream-level throughput. By continuously analyzing this data, Google was able to fine-tune congestion control algorithms and handshake parameters for different services and regions. For instance, on YouTube, Google optimized congestion control to prioritize low-latency delivery of initial video segments while adapting buffer management to account for varying network quality.

The integration of QUIC also brought security enhancements to Google's services. By embedding TLS 1.3 directly into the transport layer, QUIC ensured that all user connections were encrypted by default, reducing the risk of interception and man-in-the-middle attacks. Google further hardened its QUIC deployment by employing advanced cryptographic techniques, such as forward secrecy and session resumption via secure tickets. The combination of transport and application-level encryption helped Google comply with evolving data protection regulations and improved trust among users concerned about online privacy.

Scaling QUIC to Google's global user base was not without challenges. Engineers had to account for diverse network environments, from high-capacity fiber links in urban centers to congested and lossy mobile networks in rural areas. To address these challenges, Google experimented with different congestion control algorithms, eventually adopting BBR for many QUIC deployments. BBR's model-based approach to bandwidth estimation allowed Google to achieve high throughput and low latency even on links where packet loss was unrelated to congestion.

Google's efforts to deploy QUIC at scale also involved active participation in the IETF QUIC Working Group. By sharing performance data and lessons learned from production deployments, Google contributed to the refinement of the QUIC specification, helping ensure that the standardized protocol would be applicable to a wide variety of use cases beyond Google's own ecosystem. This collaborative approach laid the foundation for QUIC's eventual adoption by other tech giants, cloud providers, and open-source communities.

The impact of QUIC at Google scale extended beyond direct performance improvements. By reducing infrastructure resource usage through more efficient congestion control and stream multiplexing, Google achieved cost savings in terms of server CPU utilization and bandwidth consumption. Services like Google Ads also benefited from faster connection setup times, which contributed to more responsive bidding and ad-serving processes, translating into tangible revenue gains.

In deploying QUIC across such a vast and complex infrastructure, Google demonstrated the viability of a transport protocol that prioritizes speed, security, and adaptability. The company's ability to integrate QUIC into products used daily by billions of people has set a new standard for internet transport, influencing how modern applications are built and how networks are engineered to meet the demands of a mobile-first, globally connected world. Through its leadership in QUIC development and deployment, Google has redefined what is possible in transport-layer innovation, setting the stage for a new generation of low-latency, secure, and resilient internet applications.

Future Extensions and Innovations

As QUIC becomes firmly established as a foundational transport protocol for the modern internet, the protocol's inherent modularity and extensibility continue to inspire new innovations and experimental extensions. The next chapter in QUIC's evolution will likely be defined by its adaptability to emerging technologies and use cases that push the boundaries of traditional network demands. Researchers, engineers, and standardization bodies are actively exploring ways to expand QUIC's capabilities, making it more versatile, efficient, and responsive to the rapidly changing digital landscape.

One of the most anticipated innovations is multipath QUIC (MP-QUIC), a set of extensions designed to enable the simultaneous use of multiple network paths within a single QUIC connection. Unlike traditional single-path transport models, MP-QUIC allows data to flow across several interfaces, such as Wi-Fi, 5G, or satellite links, in parallel. This provides greater resilience to path failures and offers opportunities for increased throughput and load balancing. MP-QUIC is especially promising for mobile devices and edge computing environments, where clients often have access to multiple network interfaces. By intelligently distributing traffic based on path characteristics like latency and available bandwidth, MP-QUIC aims to enhance performance and reliability for real-time applications such as video conferencing, multiplayer gaming, and mission-critical industrial IoT systems.

Another area of active development is support for forward error correction (FEC) within QUIC. In networks prone to burst losses, such as wireless or satellite environments, FEC schemes can proactively introduce redundancy into transmissions, allowing receivers to recover from packet loss without waiting for retransmissions. While FEC incurs additional overhead, it can reduce latency and improve application responsiveness in scenarios where retransmission delays are unacceptable. Experimental QUIC extensions that incorporate lightweight FEC mechanisms are being evaluated for applications like live media streaming, where maintaining smooth playback is critical even under variable network conditions.

Beyond transport-level extensions, QUIC is also being considered as a substrate for entirely new application protocols. While HTTP/3 has been the most visible use case for QUIC, the protocol's stream-based architecture is flexible enough to support other protocols as well. DNS-over-QUIC (DoQ) is one such emerging standard that leverages QUIC's encryption and multiplexing to secure and accelerate domain name resolution. Similarly, researchers are exploring how QUIC could be adapted to support secure versions of messaging protocols, real-time telemetry systems, and even blockchain synchronization mechanisms. These innovations demonstrate how QUIC's versatility can simplify protocol design by handling congestion control, loss recovery, and encryption at the transport layer.

In the realm of security, future QUIC extensions will likely focus on enhancing privacy and resisting emerging threats. For example, the integration of Encrypted Client Hello (ECH) with QUIC is under active discussion. ECH addresses the privacy gap left by the exposure of the server name indication (SNI) in TLS handshakes, preventing passive observers from learning which websites or services a user is attempting to access. Combining ECH with QUIC will strengthen the protocol's resistance to censorship and surveillance, making it more attractive for privacy-sensitive applications and users operating under restrictive regimes.

Another promising direction for innovation is the integration of post-quantum cryptography (PQC) into QUIC's handshake mechanisms. As advances in quantum computing threaten traditional cryptographic algorithms, the development of quantum-resistant key exchange and encryption algorithms is gaining urgency. The modular nature of QUIC's handshake, which already embeds TLS 1.3, provides a flexible framework for adopting hybrid or fully post-quantum cryptographic primitives. Early experiments are already underway to assess the performance and security implications of such integrations, ensuring that QUIC remains future-proof against the eventual rise of quantum adversaries.

Performance optimizations will continue to be a focus of future QUIC extensions, particularly in specialized environments such as data centers. Data center networks, characterized by ultra-low latencies and high-throughput workloads, present unique challenges for transport protocols. Emerging proposals suggest fine-grained congestion control schemes, lower-latency loss recovery strategies, and adjustments to packet pacing behavior tailored to high-bandwidth, low-delay contexts. These optimizations could allow QUIC to replace TCP even in environments where microsecond-level latencies are the norm, extending the protocol's reach into the backbone of cloud infrastructure.

The growing popularity of edge computing and distributed AI workloads also calls for transport innovations at the application layer. Future QUIC extensions may introduce mechanisms for dynamic stream prioritization, allowing applications to signal changes in stream importance based on real-time workload requirements. For example, AI inference pipelines operating at the edge could prioritize control messages or time-sensitive data streams while relegating bulk data transfers to lower-priority streams, ensuring that latency-sensitive operations are not delayed by less critical traffic.

Telemetry and observability enhancements are another promising area for QUIC's future development. While QUIC's encryption protects transport metadata from intermediaries, it also limits traditional network operators' ability to monitor and optimize traffic. Future extensions may include privacy-preserving telemetry mechanisms that allow operators and application developers to gain insights into connection quality, path characteristics, and congestion signals without compromising end-user privacy. Such tools could enable more sophisticated traffic engineering strategies and improve automated network optimization in complex, multi-hop environments.

Energy efficiency is also emerging as a priority in protocol design, particularly as enterprises and cloud providers seek to reduce their carbon footprint. QUIC's user-space implementation already offers efficiency gains over kernel-based TCP stacks, but future extensions could further reduce CPU utilization and energy consumption. For example, algorithms that dynamically adjust retransmission strategies, idle connection behavior, and stream lifetimes based on real-time energy profiles are being considered as ways to minimize power usage in edge devices and data center workloads alike.

Finally, the standardization process itself will continue to play a critical role in shaping QUIC's future. The IETF and other industry forums are expected to expand QUIC's specifications to accommodate new use cases while maintaining interoperability and backward compatibility. Open-source communities and major tech companies will continue to contribute experimental implementations and performance data, accelerating the feedback loop that has been instrumental to QUIC's success thus far.

The future of QUIC is one of continuous innovation, with a growing ecosystem of extensions and research projects poised to expand the protocol's capabilities. As global network architectures become more diverse and applications place increasing demands on transport layers, QUIC's flexibility ensures that it will remain at the forefront of next-generation internet infrastructure. From multipath connectivity and privacy-enhancing features to quantum-resilient security and energy-aware transport mechanisms, the next wave of QUIC advancements promises to address the evolving challenges and opportunities of the modern digital world.

Competing Protocols and Alternatives

While QUIC has gained significant momentum as a modern transport protocol, it is not the only option under consideration by researchers, engineers, and enterprises seeking to improve performance, security, and reliability in their networks. A variety of competing protocols and alternatives have emerged or evolved alongside QUIC, each with its own set of strengths, limitations, and targeted use cases.

Understanding these competing protocols is critical to appreciating QUIC's role in the broader context of transport-layer innovation, where diverse applications and network conditions demand different solutions.

TCP, the long-standing backbone of internet transport, remains QUIC's most direct competitor. Despite its age, TCP has proven remarkably resilient, benefiting from decades of research, optimization, and hardware support. TCP continues to dominate in many environments, particularly where legacy infrastructure and backward compatibility remain critical. Enhancements such as TCP Fast Open (TFO), selective acknowledgments (SACK), window scaling, and Explicit Congestion Notification (ECN) have extended TCP's lifespan, making it suitable for a wide range of applications. However, TCP's reliance on in-order delivery and its susceptibility to head-of-line blocking continue to be pain points, especially for multiplexed application protocols such as HTTP/2.

Another notable alternative to QUIC is SCTP (Stream Control Transmission Protocol), which was originally developed to address some of TCP's limitations, such as its lack of native multistreaming and message-oriented semantics. SCTP supports multiple independent streams within a single association, avoiding head-of-line blocking across streams. Additionally, SCTP includes built-in support for multihoming, enabling a connection to span multiple IP addresses for improved redundancy. Despite these advantages, SCTP has seen limited deployment on the public internet due to firewall and middlebox incompatibilities, as many networks are optimized for TCP and UDP traffic. SCTP has found a niche in telecommunications signaling, particularly for transporting SS7 messages over IP networks, but has not achieved widespread adoption for general-purpose internet applications.

DCCP (Datagram Congestion Control Protocol) is another lesser-known competitor that aims to combine features of UDP's message-oriented model with built-in congestion control. Designed for applications such as streaming media, online gaming, and VoIP, DCCP seeks to provide a middle ground between the reliability of TCP and the low-overhead characteristics of UDP. DCCP supports various congestion control algorithms and allows applications to trade off reliability for latency, making it suitable for delay-sensitive traffic. However, like SCTP, DCCP faces deployment barriers related to middlebox traversal and limited operating system support, which have curtailed its broader adoption.

On the application layer, HTTP/2 over TCP has served as QUIC's primary alternative for web transport. HTTP/2 introduced multiplexing, header compression, and server push, delivering significant performance improvements over HTTP/1.1. However, its reliance on TCP means that HTTP/2 still inherits head-of-line blocking at the transport layer, limiting its performance in lossy or high-latency networks. This shortcoming has been a key driver for the development and adoption of HTTP/3, which replaces TCP with QUIC as the underlying transport.

Beyond traditional transport protocols, proprietary solutions have also emerged as alternatives to QUIC in specific use cases. For instance, Google's internal gQUIC protocol, the precursor to IETF QUIC, was deployed across its ecosystem before standardization efforts led to the adoption of the broader IETF version. Similarly, large technology companies and content delivery networks have experimented with custom UDP-based transport layers optimized for video delivery, real-time applications, and large-scale web services. These proprietary protocols often integrate closely with application-layer logic, providing tailored optimizations but lacking the broad interoperability of standardized solutions like QUIC.

Multipath TCP (MPTCP) is another notable alternative designed to address limitations in single-path TCP. MPTCP enables the simultaneous use of multiple network interfaces, such as Wi-Fi and cellular, to improve resilience and throughput for a single application session. By distributing traffic across multiple paths, MPTCP can provide redundancy against link failures and optimize performance based on path characteristics. MPTCP has been deployed in mobile networks and data centers but remains constrained by TCP's in-order delivery model and the complexities of middlebox traversal. While QUIC's emerging multipath extensions aim to offer similar benefits, MPTCP remains a viable option in environments where TCP-based solutions are deeply entrenched.

Emerging transport-layer protocols like RINA (Recursive InterNetwork Architecture) propose radical departures from the traditional TCP/IP model. RINA advocates for a single unified protocol structure that recurses across layers, replacing both IP and TCP with a more flexible and modular framework. While RINA remains largely in the research phase, its vision of eliminating layering overhead and enabling native Quality of Service (QoS) has attracted attention from academia and experimental networks. However, the challenges of overhauling the deeply embedded TCP/IP stack across the global internet have so far limited RINA to testbeds and niche applications.

The evolution of peer-to-peer (P2P) networks has also given rise to specialized transport protocols designed to operate efficiently in decentralized environments. Protocols like libp2p, used in IPFS and other distributed systems, offer pluggable transport layers that can operate over TCP, QUIC, WebRTC, and other substrates. Libp2p's modular design supports dynamic protocol negotiation, peer discovery, and NAT traversal, making it well-suited for blockchain networks, distributed file storage, and other decentralized applications. QUIC's adoption in libp2p-based projects reflects its growing influence, but alternative transports remain viable depending on the deployment scenario and application needs.

WebRTC is another competing protocol that, while designed primarily for real-time media and peer-to-peer communication, includes a data channel feature built on top of SCTP over DTLS over UDP. WebRTC data channels provide unordered and unreliable delivery options that are attractive for interactive applications such as online games and live collaboration tools. However, WebRTC's focus on browser-based communication and its reliance on signaling frameworks like SDP make it less suitable as a general-purpose transport protocol compared to QUIC.

The ongoing development of transport protocols highlights the diversity of requirements and environments across the internet. While QUIC offers a compelling combination of reduced latency, multiplexing, built-in encryption, and user-space implementation, other protocols continue to thrive in specific niches. TCP and HTTP/2 remain dominant in many legacy systems, SCTP is entrenched in telecommunications, and specialized solutions like MPTCP, DCCP, and WebRTC continue to serve unique roles where QUIC's features may not fully align with application constraints.

Ultimately, the transport protocol landscape is one of coexistence rather than competition alone. As applications evolve and new networking paradigms emerge, organizations will continue to weigh the trade-offs between interoperability, performance, and deployment complexity. QUIC's flexibility positions it as a strong contender for the next generation of internet services, but the ongoing refinement and niche adoption of alternative protocols ensure that innovation at the transport layer will remain dynamic and multi-faceted for years to come.

QUIC and the Broader Internet Ecosystem

The rise of QUIC represents not just the advancement of a single transport protocol but a fundamental shift in how the broader internet ecosystem operates. From content delivery networks (CDNs) and cloud providers to browsers, mobile operators, and enterprise networks, QUIC's design choices are reshaping interactions across the entire stack. The protocol's combination of performance optimization, security by default, and flexibility is influencing stakeholders at every layer, altering how data moves through the internet and how applications are built to serve an increasingly global and diverse user base.

At its core, QUIC addresses long-standing inefficiencies in the transport layer that became more pronounced as the internet evolved from a best-effort network to one supporting real-time applications, high-definition streaming, cloud computing, and edge services. The introduction of encrypted transport headers, fast handshake processes, and stream multiplexing directly challenges the status quo maintained by TCP for decades. The broader internet ecosystem, accustomed to designing around TCP's limitations, is now transitioning to leverage QUIC's benefits while grappling with new considerations related to network visibility, infrastructure compatibility, and traffic management.

Browsers have been among the first major players to adopt and propagate QUIC throughout the internet. Google Chrome and Mozilla Firefox were early adopters, with Microsoft Edge and Apple's Safari following closely behind. This widespread browser support has pushed content providers and web application developers to enable HTTP/3, which runs atop QUIC, to improve page load times and reduce latency. As browsers drive user traffic through QUIC, web servers and CDNs have accelerated their efforts to deploy QUIC-compatible endpoints, creating a virtuous cycle where client and server ecosystems reinforce each other's progress.

CDNs, tasked with bringing content closer to end users, have been at the forefront of QUIC's adoption. Cloudflare, Akamai, Fastly, and others have integrated QUIC into their edge networks, enabling faster content delivery and improving reliability in congested or lossy network conditions. For CDNs, QUIC's reduced handshake latency translates into faster time-to-first-byte (TTFB) metrics, while multiplexing ensures that a single lost packet does not delay other streams, critical for delivering complex web pages composed of multiple assets. By encrypting transport metadata, QUIC also helps CDN providers enhance user privacy, aligning with the growing emphasis on data protection regulations such as GDPR and CCPA.

Cloud service providers like Google Cloud, AWS, and Microsoft Azure have incorporated QUIC into their load balancing and application delivery solutions, influencing how backend services communicate internally and how external client traffic is processed. In distributed microservice architectures common in cloud-native environments, QUIC's multiplexing and connection migration capabilities offer benefits for service-to-service communication, particularly when paired with service mesh frameworks. These benefits extend to APIs, which increasingly rely on HTTP/3 for efficient and secure interactions between clients and cloud-hosted backends.

Network operators, including mobile and fixed-line ISPs, are navigating both opportunities and challenges as QUIC adoption grows. On one hand, QUIC improves the quality of experience for end users by reducing connection setup times and enhancing performance under varying network conditions. On the other hand, QUIC's encryption of transport headers complicates traditional traffic engineering practices that rely on visibility into transport-layer metadata. ISPs must now develop new tools and methodologies to monitor and optimize encrypted traffic flows, often focusing on endpoint telemetry, flow-level metrics, and aggregated statistics to maintain network health without compromising user privacy.

In the enterprise space, organizations adopting QUIC benefit from improved security and performance in remote work scenarios. With employees accessing cloud applications and internal systems over VPNs or direct internet connections, QUIC reduces session startup times and mitigates performance degradation during network transitions, such as switching from office Wi-Fi to mobile networks. Enterprises integrating Zero Trust Network Access (ZTNA) and SD-WAN solutions are also aligning with QUIC's principles, as its transport-layer encryption and connection migration capabilities support the dynamic, identity-centric access models required by modern IT infrastructures.

The IoT ecosystem is also being impacted by QUIC's expansion. Many IoT devices operate on constrained networks where low power consumption and resilience to packet loss are crucial. QUIC's efficient handshake and robust congestion control algorithms make it an attractive option for secure telemetry and command-and-control data transfer between devices and cloud services. In industries such as healthcare, manufacturing, and logistics, QUIC is being evaluated for use in IoT deployments where reliable, low-latency communication is paramount.

Security practitioners are engaging with QUIC's impact on network visibility and threat detection. While QUIC's encryption improves privacy and security for legitimate users, it also limits the ability of traditional intrusion detection and prevention systems (IDPS) to inspect traffic for anomalies. As a result, organizations are adapting their security models to rely more heavily on endpoint-based defenses, behavioral analysis, and machine learning to detect malicious activity that may be hidden within QUIC-encrypted sessions. At the same time, QUIC's mandatory TLS 1.3 encryption raises the baseline security for all internet users, reducing exposure to common threats such as downgrade attacks or unauthorized data inspection.

The broader research community has taken a keen interest in QUIC as well. Universities and network laboratories are leveraging open-source QUIC implementations to explore new transport-layer features, congestion control algorithms, and security enhancements. QUIC's user-space design accelerates experimentation, allowing researchers to prototype extensions for areas such as multipath transport, forward error correction, and privacy-preserving telemetry. The collaborative feedback loop between academia, industry, and standards bodies such as the IETF ensures that QUIC's evolution remains informed by real-world deployment insights and cutting-edge research.

Furthermore, QUIC is influencing regulatory and policy discussions about the future of internet protocols. As encrypted transport layers like QUIC become the norm, regulators are considering how to balance the benefits of stronger user privacy with the operational needs of network operators and public safety agencies. These debates are shaping guidance on lawful intercept capabilities, network neutrality, and best practices for encrypted traffic management, underscoring how deeply transport-layer innovations can impact internet governance.

Ultimately, QUIC is reshaping the dynamics of the global internet ecosystem by redefining how speed, security, and adaptability are achieved at the transport layer. It is fostering a more decentralized, privacy-respecting, and performance-driven internet, where applications are empowered to optimize user experience across increasingly diverse network environments. As more stakeholders adopt QUIC and build complementary tools and services around it, the protocol's role as a catalyst for broader technological and organizational change is becoming clear. Its success demonstrates that innovation at the foundational layers of the internet continues to be essential to meeting the demands of the modern digital world.

QUIC's Role in Shaping Next-Gen Applications

As the digital world moves into an era defined by highly interactive, real-time, and distributed applications, QUIC is emerging as a critical enabler of next-generation services and platforms. The protocol's architecture offers solutions to many transport-layer limitations that have historically constrained application performance and reliability. With its reduced handshake latency, built-in encryption, support for multiplexed streams, and resilience to network variability, QUIC is fundamentally influencing how developers design and deploy modern applications across industries.

One of the most noticeable ways QUIC is shaping next-gen applications is by addressing the persistent demand for low-latency interactions. Applications such as multiplayer games, real-time collaboration tools, and live streaming platforms depend on fast and reliable communication to provide a seamless user experience. Traditional transport protocols, particularly TCP, often introduce delays due to connection setup times and head-of-line blocking. QUIC's ability to establish encrypted connections with a single round trip—or zero round trips when session resumption is used—helps applications deliver faster responses, reducing wait times for end users and ensuring that interactive workflows remain fluid. This benefit is particularly significant in environments like mobile networks, where network conditions fluctuate and users often switch between Wi-Fi, 5G, and other access networks.

The emergence of immersive technologies, such as augmented reality (AR) and virtual reality (VR), further underscores the importance of transport protocols like QUIC. These applications require ultra-low-latency data transmission and consistent throughput to render real-time environments without lag or degradation. QUIC's connection migration capabilities allow AR and VR sessions to persist across changing network interfaces, such as when a user moves from one wireless access point to another, preserving session continuity without noticeable interruptions. Additionally, QUIC's multiplexing feature enables developers to manage different data types—such as position tracking, audio streams, and video feeds—within a single connection while preventing one stream from stalling others due to packet loss.

The cloud-native application paradigm, where services are increasingly distributed across microservice architectures and edge locations, is also benefiting from QUIC. In cloud-native deployments, services must frequently communicate across data centers, regions, and edge nodes. QUIC's ability to reduce handshake overhead and optimize bandwidth utilization is crucial in minimizing inter-service latency and maintaining efficient communication in these dynamic environments. For instance, service meshes that facilitate secure communication between microservices are integrating QUIC to improve throughput and latency for workloads that must scale horizontally and operate across diverse network conditions.

E-commerce and financial applications are leveraging QUIC to enhance both performance and security. For online retailers, faster page loads and checkout processes directly influence conversion rates and customer satisfaction. QUIC, by accelerating the delivery of web assets through HTTP/3 and reducing time-to-first-byte, allows e-commerce platforms to provide snappier user experiences, particularly in mobile-first markets where consumers expect immediate responsiveness. In financial services, where transaction integrity and speed are paramount, QUIC's integration of TLS 1.3 encryption ensures that data in transit is protected while enabling faster transaction processing through lower latency connections.

Real-time communication platforms, including voice over IP (VoIP), video conferencing, and instant messaging services, are increasingly turning to QUIC to deliver smoother interactions. For example, video conferencing platforms must manage multiple media streams—audio, video, screen sharing, and chat—concurrently within a session. QUIC's multiplexing architecture allows these streams to operate independently, preventing a minor loss in one stream from cascading into performance issues across others. Moreover, QUIC's congestion control mechanisms, especially when paired with algorithms like BBR, optimize media delivery in networks with variable conditions, maintaining consistent audio and video quality even when packet loss or jitter is present.

Edge computing is another frontier where QUIC is playing a pivotal role in shaping next-generation applications. As computation moves closer to users and devices to reduce latency and network load, edge nodes require efficient transport protocols to communicate with cloud data centers, IoT devices, and end-user applications. QUIC's support for connection migration, encryption, and multiplexed streams enables edge platforms to efficiently manage telemetry, control signals, and application data within a unified transport layer. This is vital for use cases such as smart cities, where edge nodes orchestrate traffic management systems, public safety networks, and environmental sensors that depend on real-time data flow.

AI-driven applications are also finding synergies with QUIC's capabilities. Machine learning workloads that require frequent communication between distributed nodes, such as federated learning or model-serving frameworks, benefit from QUIC's reduced handshake latency and efficient bandwidth usage. As AI models are increasingly deployed at the edge for real-time inference, QUIC facilitates secure and low-latency transport between inference nodes and data sources. Additionally, AI-driven applications that deliver personalized experiences, such as recommendation engines or virtual assistants, can leverage QUIC's stream prioritization to dynamically adjust data delivery based on real-time user interactions and contextual signals.

The gaming industry, both in cloud gaming and multiplayer scenarios, is actively embracing QUIC to address transport-layer challenges. In cloud gaming, where gameplay is rendered on remote servers and streamed to client devices, minimizing latency is critical to preserving responsiveness and competitive fairness. QUIC's lower connection setup time and resilience to packet loss reduce input lag and improve the overall gaming experience. For multiplayer games, QUIC enables developers to create session architectures that seamlessly handle player disconnections and network switches, minimizing disruption when users experience temporary connectivity issues or switch between network interfaces mid-game.

Security-centric applications are another area where QUIC is making a substantial impact. Applications that handle sensitive user data, such as telehealth platforms, government services, or encrypted messaging apps, are integrating QUIC to ensure that encryption is enforced by default and that transport-layer metadata remains protected from passive observers. The protocol's encryption of transport headers limits the potential for traffic analysis and helps protect user privacy, aligning with the increasing demand for secure and compliant applications under regulations such as GDPR and HIPAA.

In decentralized and peer-to-peer systems, such as blockchain networks and distributed file storage platforms, QUIC's user-space implementation and flexibility allow developers to integrate it as a modular transport option. Distributed applications benefit from QUIC's NAT traversal capabilities and stream multiplexing, which simplify peer discovery and data synchronization between nodes. Additionally, QUIC's extensibility opens the door to experiment with emerging features like multipath transport and forward error correction, enhancing resilience and performance in complex, heterogeneous network environments.

The growing ecosystem of QUIC-based libraries and open-source implementations further empowers application developers to tailor the protocol to the specific needs of their platforms. Whether optimizing for minimal power consumption in IoT devices or maximizing throughput in cloud-native applications, QUIC offers a customizable transport layer that adapts to a variety of performance and security requirements.

As digital experiences continue to evolve toward greater interactivity, personalization, and real-time responsiveness, QUIC is establishing itself as a key enabler of next-generation applications. Its influence extends far beyond the web, reshaping how applications are architected to deliver seamless, secure, and adaptive experiences across diverse network conditions. By removing the bottlenecks and vulnerabilities inherent to older transport protocols, QUIC is empowering developers to build innovative applications that meet the expectations of modern users and the demands of a connected world.

The Road Ahead: QUIC's Lasting Legacy

As QUIC continues to shape the landscape of modern internet communications, its long-term impact is becoming increasingly evident across industries, technologies, and digital experiences. What began as an experimental transport protocol aimed at addressing specific limitations in TCP has grown into a transformative force influencing how applications are designed, how networks operate, and how users interact with the digital world. QUIC's legacy will not be defined solely by its technical specifications but by the new paradigms it has introduced and the waves of innovation it has inspired across the global internet ecosystem.

One of the most profound aspects of QUIC's legacy is the normalization of security by design. QUIC has permanently raised the bar by integrating TLS 1.3 encryption into the transport layer itself, making encrypted-by-default communication a new standard. By encrypting both payload and transport metadata, QUIC prioritizes user privacy and protects applications from common threats such as passive surveillance and session hijacking. This design choice has reverberated across the internet, encouraging a broader shift toward default encryption in protocols and services beyond just QUIC. The expectation that security should be built into every layer of the stack is becoming more widely accepted, reshaping how developers and network architects think about security.

Equally significant is how QUIC has altered expectations around performance and efficiency. By reducing handshake latency, eliminating head-of-line blocking, and providing built-in multiplexing, QUIC has reset what developers and users anticipate in terms of application responsiveness. Whether users are loading a complex web page, engaging in a video call, or participating in an online game, the seamless, low-latency experience that QUIC enables is redefining user satisfaction benchmarks. These improvements are particularly impactful in mobile-first markets and emerging economies, where network conditions may be less stable and where every millisecond saved has a tangible effect on user engagement and accessibility.

The influence of QUIC has also reshaped the transport protocol development process itself. Historically, innovations at the transport layer were slow to materialize, often constrained by legacy compatibility requirements and the need to integrate deeply with operating system kernels. QUIC's user-space implementation model has proven that transport protocols can be agile, adaptable, and customizable. Developers can now iterate on congestion control algorithms, handshake optimizations, and transport features without waiting for kernel-level changes, accelerating the pace of innovation. This agility is inspiring a new wave of transport-layer experimentation and reinforcing the idea that transport protocols can evolve in tandem with modern application requirements.

QUIC's legacy is also evident in the rise of HTTP/3, the latest evolution of the web's most critical application-layer protocol. HTTP/3, built atop QUIC, brings web transport into a new era characterized by faster page loads, smoother streaming, and improved resilience to packet loss. The broad adoption of HTTP/3 by browsers, CDNs, and major web services demonstrates how tightly coupled QUIC has become with the fabric of the modern internet. As more websites and platforms enable HTTP/3, QUIC's design choices directly influence how web content is delivered, consumed, and optimized globally.

Beyond its direct applications, QUIC has initiated important conversations about transparency, privacy, and control in network operations. With most transport headers encrypted, traditional middlebox-based traffic management has become more challenging, forcing a reevaluation of how networks monitor and optimize encrypted traffic flows. This shift is leading to the development of new telemetry standards, endpoint-based observability solutions, and privacy-preserving network management techniques. QUIC has accelerated the industry's move toward balancing operational needs with stronger privacy guarantees, influencing how enterprises, ISPs, and regulators approach the future of internet infrastructure.

QUIC's impact extends deeply into specialized industries and use cases. In cloud-native environments, QUIC is now a key enabler of service-to-service communication, microservice architectures, and distributed applications that operate across multiple data centers and edge nodes. Its stream multiplexing and connection migration features have proven valuable in supporting highly scalable applications that demand consistent performance in dynamic and decentralized environments. In sectors such as finance, healthcare, and logistics, where real-time data transfer and regulatory compliance are critical, QUIC's security and performance attributes are helping organizations meet stringent service-level agreements and privacy mandates.

The legacy of QUIC is not limited to traditional enterprise and web contexts. It is influencing emerging technologies such as 5G, IoT, and edge computing. In the 5G ecosystem, where ultra-low-latency and high-bandwidth communication is essential, QUIC's ability to migrate sessions across changing IP addresses and to maintain connection stability in mobile scenarios complements the goals of next-generation wireless networks. In IoT deployments, where resource-constrained devices must securely transmit data over unreliable networks, QUIC's reduced handshake overhead and transport-layer encryption enable more efficient and secure communications.

QUIC has also catalyzed innovation in multipath transport, forward error correction, and AI-assisted congestion control. As developers explore extensions and enhancements to the protocol, QUIC is serving as a platform for next-generation features that promise even greater adaptability, robustness, and intelligence in transport-layer behavior. Experimental initiatives such as multipath QUIC (MP-QUIC) are demonstrating how QUIC's foundation can be expanded to fully leverage multiple network interfaces for improved redundancy and performance, further solidifying its role as a future-proof protocol.

Perhaps one of the most enduring elements of QUIC's legacy is its contribution to the open internet ethos. By engaging deeply with the IETF and the broader open-source community, the creators of QUIC ensured that the protocol would not remain a proprietary solution but would become a standardized, globally accessible technology. This commitment to openness has fostered widespread collaboration, interoperability testing, and transparent development processes that benefit organizations of all sizes. QUIC's open standardization has enabled independent developers, small businesses, and research institutions to experiment with and deploy the protocol alongside the world's largest tech companies.

As QUIC continues to evolve, its lasting legacy will be felt not just in the services that implement it but in the mindset it has instilled across the internet industry. QUIC has shown that transport protocols can be secure by default, fast without sacrificing resilience, and modular enough to adapt to both current and future demands. It has challenged entrenched assumptions about what is possible at the transport layer and has opened doors for a new generation of engineers to reimagine how data flows across networks.

The road ahead for QUIC is one of continued expansion and influence. From global content delivery to decentralized applications and next-generation wireless networks, QUIC's principles will continue to shape the evolution of internet transport for years to come. Its legacy is that of a protocol that not only fixed the shortcomings of its predecessors but also laid the foundation for a more secure, responsive, and flexible internet. The story of QUIC is ultimately the story of how modern connectivity must continually adapt to the accelerating demands of an interconnected world, and how innovation at even the deepest layers of the internet can have ripple effects that touch every user, application, and network on the planet.

www.ingramcontent.com/pod-product-compliance
Lightning Source LLC
LaVergne TN
LVHW022316060326
832902LV00020B/3492